D0852118

Wars of Consolidation
and Expansion

The
MILITARY HISTORY
of the
UNITED STATES

Christopher Chant

Wars of Consolidation and Expansion

MARSHALL CAVENDISH
NEW YORK · LONDON · TORONTO · SYDNEY

Library Edition Published 1992

© Marshall Cavendish Limited 1992

Published by
Marshall Cavendish Corporation
2415 Jerusalem Avenue
PO Box 587
North Bellmore
New York 11710

Series created by Graham Beehag Book Design

Series Editor	Maggi McCormick
Consultant Editors	James R. Arnold
	Roberta Wiener
Sub Editor	Julie Cairns
Designer	Graham Beehag
Illustrators	John Batchelor
	Steve Lucas
	Terry Forest
	Colette Brownrigg
Indexer	Mark Dartford

Library of Congress Cataloging-in-Publication Data

Chant, Christopher.
   The Military History of the United States / Christopher Chant –
Library ed.
      p. cm.
   Includes bibliographical references and index.
   Summary: Surveys the wars that have directly influenced the
   United States., from the Revolutionary War through the Cold War.
   ISBN 1-85435-354-3 ISBN 1-85435-361-9 (set)
   1. United States - History, Military - Juvenile literature.
   [1. United States - History, Military.] I. Title.
   t181.C52 1991
   973 - dc20   90 - 19547
                                           CIP
                                           AC

Printed in Singapore by Times Offset PTE Ltd
Bund in the United States

The publishers wish to thank the following organizations
who have supplied photographs:

The National Archives, Washington. United States
Navy, United States Marines, United States Army,
United States Air Force, Department of Defense,
Library of Congress, The Smithsonian Institution.

The publishers gratefully thank the U.S. Army Military
History Institute, Carlisle Barracks, PA. for the use of
archive material for the following witness accounts:

Page 18
A collection of items from *History of Pittsfield
Massachusetts* by Joseph E. Smith, (Boston 1869);
The Military Annals of Lancaster Massachusetts by
Harry S. Nourse, (Lancaster 1889); and *The Life of
Major John Paterson* by Thomas Egleston, (New York
1898).

Page 41
History of the Late War in the Western Country by
Robert Breckenridge McAfee, (Lexington, 1816).

Page 109
The War in Florida by a Staff Officer by Woodburne
Potter, (Baltimore, 1836).

Page 110
Notices of Florida: The Campaign by M. M. Cohen
(New York, 1836).

Page 117
From *Order of the Indian Wars Collection*, U.S. Army
Military History Institute, Carlisle Barracks, PA.

Page 118
Letters From the Frontiers by Major General George
A. McCall, (Philadelphia, 1868).

Contents

In 1783 the Revolutionary War ended and the United States of America became a sovereign nation as the last British troops were evacuated from New York. Even before the final withdrawal, the Continental Congress had started to demobilize its army, and various state militia units had already returned home.

It was a time for reflection on the reasons why the United States had won the Revolutionary War, and how best to maintain the new country as an independent state. George Washington, looking at the American difficulties throughout the eight years of the Revolutionary War, could explain the American victory only through the intervention of "Divine Providence" on the side of the 13 divided states to defeat Great Britain, at that time the most powerful country in the world. Historical hindsight suggests a number of more practical reasons including British strategic mistakes (especially in 1776-77 and 1780),

Washington's leadership and the support provided by the French.

The "Generalship" Factor

All these factors contributed to the American victory, but there are a number of other matters that should be taken into account. Washington, for example, was not responsible for several of the decisive American victories of the war, so the generalship of Benedict Arnold, Nathanael Greene, Henry Knox and Daniel Morgan were also vitally important. The operational and tactical generalship of such leaders would have been useless without the dedication of the average officer and soldier of the Continental Army. Their commitment is shown by the way that the men drove themselves through the hardships of the march on Quebec, the crossing of the

George Washington
For further references see pages
7,8,9,13,14,15,20,22,24-,26,29,42,49,*54*,55,89,9-1,100

The qualities that made George Washington a great general were the same ones that inspired all sixty nine members of the first Electoral College to vote for him in February 1789, to elect him as the first President of the United States of America. In his two terms as president, Washington faced problems as difficult as those he met as commander-in-chief of the Continental Army in the Revolutionary War.

Continental Congress
For further references see pages
9,49,50,54,55,*88*,89,90

Continental Army
For further references
see pages
6,9,20,23,49,54

By the end of the 18th century, the sword had only limited practical use on the battlefield, except in the hands of the cavalry. Even so, the weapon was widely used especially as a distinguishing mark for officers. These European swords are an assortment used in the United States.

Delaware River before the Battle of Trenton, the dire winters at Valley Forge and Morristown, and Greene's forced marches in the southern campaign. The men on the British side often showed great heroism and determination, but they never needed the same degree of dedication that the American soldiers needed and possessed.

This dedication was also displayed by the frequently misunderstood militiamen. Some historians have said that the militia units were useless and that it was the men of the Continental Army who won the war. Others claim that the militiamen were the true citizen-soldiers who won the war. The truth lies somewhere between these two extreme views: the militiamen often made great contributions, though they would have counted for relatively little without the existence of the Continental Army as the permanent core around which the militia units could gather. The fact that militia units could, and did, appear wherever and whenever they were needed often negated the British victories over the Continental Army. This loyalty emphasizes the fact that another key factor in the American victory was the control established over the countryside by patriots before the war had even started. The British were therefore faced with the immensely difficult task of defeating not just an armed enemy in the field. Regardless of the numbers of loyalists that rallied to the British cause, the countryside was filled with those who wanted an independent America.

The Importance of French Support

Even so, only French aid enabled the Americans to win. Most of the small arms, bayonets, and cannon used by the Continental Army came from France. French naval power had diverted British strength to other areas and hampered the British control of the seas that was so important a part of their strategic arsenal. Finally, French manpower and technical skill assured the victory at Yorktown that had been created by Washington's strategic skill.

As the dust of the war began to settle, some far-sighted Americans began to realize that French support had been needed mainly because the American effort lacked any real central direction. Much as Americans in general might not want a strong central government, it was clear that such a government was needed for the control of a major war effort. It is hardly surprising, therefore, that when the Founding Fathers were drafting a new constitution in 1787, most of those who had commanded, or even held high administrative position, during the Revolutionary War argued in favor of a central government with a moderately strong executive and the right to levy taxes directly on the people, to call out the militia, and, most important of all in purely military terms, to "raise armies and navies."

Tactical Conclusions Difficult to Reach

At a strictly military level it was more difficult to draw firm conclusions from the Revolutionary War. No completely new tactics were developed during the war. However, by the end of the war, a practice that had begun in the French and Indian Wars (1754-60) had become standard on both sides. European line formations, with men arranged in several ranks across the front, were used in conjunction with light infantry deployed forward of the main body as skirmishers. Ironically, the British adopted the American concept of skirmishers and fighting from behind cover wherever possible. The American army meanwhile tried to match the British

discipline of fighting in ranks. Militia officers praised the rifle as a weapon that provided the accurate long-range fire. It had proved decisive in actions such as Saratoga and King's Mountain, both fought in hilly and wooded terrain. More sensible men pointed out that the rifle was slow to reload and also lacked a bayonet, which made it less useful than the smooth-bore musket for most military actions.

In the post-war assessment of the United States' future army requirements, some supported a large regular army. Others felt that most resources should be allocated to a militia army. As Washington saw, however, the problem did not lie with such a choice between a large regular army or large militia forces. Because of its geographical situation and political nature, the United States did not need or even want a large regular army. It needed a small professional army and comparatively large militia forces. The important thing, as Washington and others correctly saw, was that both forces should be organized and trained on similar lines to create a large and

Most of the firearms used by the Continental Army were imported. This German holster pistol, with a carved trigger tip and a carved stock is typical.

homogeneous national reserve. Such an organization would allow each state to raise and run its own militia force, but each of these "state armies" would be run according to standards decided at national level. The militia forces could be then called into effective national service in the event of war or any other national emergency. Washington and others wanted a limited form of what the French were soon to call "the nation in arms." This concept allowed political and economic freedom to be balanced by the obligation of all citizens to fight for the state when required.

In this can be seen the first step toward the "democratization of war." This ultimately led to the concepts of a national draft and, by extension, of total war waged at the national level.

Demobilization for the Continental Army

Even as the first military lessons of the Revolutionary War were being discussed in the Continental Congress and various

military headquarters, the men of the Continental Army were growing restless. Through the winter of 1782-83, the army had become impatient with its treatment by the Congress. This impatience became clear when anonymous pamphlets began to enter circulation among the officers of the garrison at Newburgh. One pamphlet urged the officers to lay down their arms if peace was declared but their pay was not settled. Another argued that the officers should refuse to fight even if the war was not ended. Washington was all too aware that his officers and men had many real grievances. In a direct approach, he offered to fight their case with the Congress. Eventually, he won a full settlement of back pay for the men, and five years' full pay for the officers in place of half pay for life. With this thorny problem settled, men started to leave the Continental Army as early as June 1783. However, it was not until September 24, just four days after the Treaty of Paris had become effective, that the Congress ordered Washington to demobilize "such parts of the Federal Army now in Service as he shall deem proper and expedient." Washington decided to keep the force facing the British in New York, but demobilized the rest of the Continental Army. When the British finally pulled out of New York, the commander-in-chief ordered that only one infantry regiment and one artillery battalion (600 men) should be kept in service to protect the major depot at West Point and some other smaller depots.

The Hamilton Committee

The Congress was meanwhile beginning its definitive survey of the type of army the United States would be needing in the future. A committee, headed by Alexander Hamilton, was to study the facts and make recommendations. The Congress was already worried that the Newburgh situation showed the army's inclination toward coercion of the states. Some feared that this tendency might lead to a military dictatorship. The Congress therefore veered toward the establishment of a militia army. It felt that a "well-regulated and disciplined militia

Alexander Hamilton

For further references see pages 13,14,21,22

New York

For further references see pages 8, *14*,15,17,53,55,*96*

President George
Washington reviews
the Western Army at
Fort Cumberland in
about 1795.

U.S. Captain, 2nd. Sublegion of the Regular Army, 1795

Under Major General "Mad Anthony" Wayne, the regular army for the wars against the Indian tribes of the Northwest was reorganized into the Legion, which was then further divided into four Sublegions. Men of the Legion's infantry wore a blue coat with red facings, and a leather cap or ordinary round hat trimmed with a roach of bearskin, a cloth band, a cockade, and a feather. By an order of September 11, 1792, the men of the 1st Sublegion wore a cap with black hair and a white band and plume; those of the 2nd Sublegion a cap with white hair and a red band and plume; those of the 3rd Sublegion a cap with black hair and a yellow band and plume; and those of the 4th Sublegion a cap with white hair and a green band and plume. Company officers wore the same headgear as their men, while field officers wore the standard cocked hat with the appropriate sublegion feather. It should be noted, however, that this was the parade dress, worn with pipe-clayed belts, polished brass and, in the case of officers, powdered wigs. In the field, however, the men reverted to the more practical fringed hunting jacket.

One of the major difficulties faced by the fledgling United States at the end of the 18th century was consolidation and control of its northwestern frontier. The local Indian tribes and the Canadian-based British both had a vested interest in spoiling American ambitions. The disputed area was potentially rich, but presented many military problems. These problems were worse in winter, as this painting of a scouting party suggests.

sufficiently armed and accoutered" was militarily adequate, avoided the expense of a regular army, and simplified the argument between those wanting a strong central government and the adherents of the present situation of loosely federated states.

Not unnaturally, Hamilton's committee turned first to Washington, who pointed out the financial and political dangers of a large regular army. He urged the creation of a citizens' militia enrolling all manpower aged between 18 and 50 years, with a volunteer militia recruited as units and trained periodically for use under national rather than state control. Washington had also correctly analyzed the British use of seapower in the Revolutionary War. He advised setting aside available funds for "building and equipping a Navy without which, in case of War we could neither protect our Commerce, nor yield that assistance to each other which, on such an extent of seacoast, our mutual safety would require." Washington also felt that a small regular army of one artillery and four infantry regiments (2,630 men) would be an asset "to awe the In-

dians, protect our Trade, prevent the encroachment of our Neighbors of Canada and the Floridas, and guard us at least from surprises; also for security of our magazines."

Key Role for the Militia

The Hamilton committee also listened to advice from other officers and to Benjamin Lincoln, the Secretary of War. It recommended a scheme based on Washington's concept, but with a more capable militia component. The committee's advice was rejected by the Congress, largely on economic grounds, although constitutional problems and the rivalry of congressional factions also contributed. The Hamilton committee then reworked its recommendations. Eventually, it came up with a plan for a larger army that would cost the Congress less. The regimental officers would be paid at a lower rate than in the original scheme. Washington maintained that a larger army for less pay was not realistic, but he admitted that the need to provide for detached service along the frontiers and coasts demanded a larger army than he had recommended. The Congress agreed with Washington on the impossibility of providing a larger army for less money. When the Hamilton committee's revised scheme was presented on October 23, the Congress refused to accept it. Matters rested there through the winter of 1783-84. Under the terms of the Articles of Confederation ratified in 1781, the "yes" vote of at least nine states was needed for the Congress to decide a number of important issues, including military affairs. During that winter, there were few times when the Congress had enough members present for a decision to be reached.

The debate about a permanent army was renewed in the spring of 1784, but it got bogged down in a dispute about state claims to the western territories. The army was then at a strength of one infantry regiment and one artillery battalion. Most of the men were provided by Massachusetts and New Hampshire, but they were unwilling to continue giving the men the additional pay they had been offered to enlist. The Congress said that it would take over responsibility for payment, but only if the New England states would vote for the permanent military establishment that was proposed. The New England representatives argued that the Congress had no mandate to maintain a standing army. At the same time, however, they were urging the Congress to use the existing army to occupy forts located in the western territories claimed by the New England states. This request met vigorous opposition from New York, which denied the New England claims to western territories (especially in the area of Oswego and Fort Niagara). New York refused to vote for a permanent military establishment unless the western forts were occupied with New York troops.

British Occupation of American Territory

The forts under claim were those controlling the Great Lakes and the upper

The northern frontier of the United States between 1783 and 1812.

THE NORTHERN FRONTIER 1783-1812

Posts in U.S. Territory held by British until 1796

Engagement with Indians

reaches of the St. Lawrence River. From east to west along the frontier between Canada and the United States, there were forts at Pointe au Fer at the northern end of Lake Champlain, Oswegatchie on the upper reaches of the St. Lawrence River, Oswego on the southern side of Lake Ontario, Fort Niagara on the northern side of the neck of land separating Lakes Ontario and Erie, Fort Miami at the western end of Lake Erie, Detroit on Lake St. Clair between Lakes Erie and Huron, and Michilimackinac on the southern side of the neck of land separating Lakes Michigan and Superior. All were in British hands at the end of the Revolutionary War, but were located in American territory as defined in the Treaty of Paris. The treaty provided for all of the forts to be handed over to the United States as rapidly as possible. The Congress agreed

that a force should be available to occupy the forts as soon as the British left them, but could not agree how and by whom the troops were to be raised. A decision was needed urgently, because the Congress was negotiating a treaty with the resident Indian tribes. They understood that, as Washington had put it, a force "to awe the Indians" would be a useful negotiating asset. But New York was deadlocked with the New England states over the issue. It was June 1784 before the matter was resolved.

On the last two days of the Congressional session, a compromise was forced through. This measure ordered the disbandment of the existing infantry regiment and artillery battalion except for 80 artillerymen to guard the arsenals at West Point and Fort Pitt. Linked to the discharge of the existing force was an ar-

The Indian tribes were suspicious of American motives as the westward expansion gathered pace. Scenes such as this, with an Indian chief forbidding the passage of an American wagon train through his territory, inevitably led to clashes. These disputes became increasingly serious as the American government moved to protect its citizens.

rangement for the enlistment of a new force. Eight companies of one infantry regiment and two companies of artillery (800 men) would become the core of a new regular army. The Congress did not require the states to supply men, suggesting instead that the states provide them from their militia units. This sidestepped many of the objections of the New England states. By not imposing a quota on Massachusetts and New Hampshire, Congress met the objections of most of the other states.

The four states which were to provide troops were Pennsylvania (260 men), Connecticut (165 men), New York (165 men) and New Jersey (110 men). The commanding officer appointed for the new force was Lieutenant Colonel Josiah Harmar of Pennsylvania. By the end of September 1784, only New Jersey and Pennsylvania had supplied their quotas by enlisting volunteers from their militia units.

Payment for Loyalists Demanded From the United States

While the United States was struggling to establish the core of a regular army, the Congress learned that the British had little intention of leaving the forts named in the Treaty of Paris. Incensed by this treaty provision, fur trading companies with interests in upper Canada (the area that is now Ottawa) had joined forces with settlers to exert political pressure. The British government had with great secrecy instructed the governor-general of Canada not to evacuate the forts without direct instruction from London. When the matter came to light, the British government said that it was retaining the forts

Friction between the Indians and American settlers in the Northwest produced a crop of increasingly bloody episodes as raid was followed by counter-raid. Much heated ''propaganda'' emerged, such as this picture entitled ''Massacre of the Christian Indians,'' claiming that ''of the number cruelly murdered by the backwoodsmen of the upper Ohio, between fifty and sixty were women and children - some of them innocent babes.''

The Indians proved themselves masters of the type of irregular warfare waged along the frontier, and this Indian war party is typical of the bands that launched many "hit and run" raids on the settlers who encroached ever more frequently on Indian lands.

because the United States had failed to implement another treaty provision. This involved the recovery of debts owed to loyalists, of whom at least 40,000 had moved into Canada after the end of the Revolutionary War.

In these circumstances, the New Jersey contingent of the new army was sent to Fort Stanwix on the upper reaches of the Mohawk River in New York to play its part in persuading the Iroquois to abandon their lands. Meanwhile, the Pennsylvania contingent was sent to Fort MacIntosh, 30 miles down the Ohio River from Fort Pitt, to play a similar role against the Delaware. Since 1660, this tribe had been drifting west from their original homes on the eastern seaboard after their defeat by the Dutch in the Esopus War. It was not until 1796 that the British finally handed over the seven frontier forts in question.

As the United States emerged from the turmoil of the Revolutionary War, it became increasingly clear that there were severe defects in the new nation's system of government. The most important were the central government's lack of an executive and a judiciary. As a result of the ratification of the Articles of Confederation, the Congress could manage to a certain extent in these two fields. Then the greatest stumbling block faced by the Congress as an instrument of central government was its lack of the legal right to levy taxes. This absence of any real central power worried many of the delegates to the Congress. They felt that the new nation did not have the strength to survive a possible civil war which they felt could break out as a result of constant bickering about the western territories. Another indication of trouble to come was rioting in Massachusetts, which started in August 1786 and continued during the winter of 1786-87. The riots were caused mainly by an economic depression, which had followed the postwar economic boom. It inflicted great hardship on back-country farmers, and mobs formed in the Massachusetts hills. They halted the judicial process completely by breaking up court meetings and harassing lawyers. In a more obviously threatening move, the mobs seemed to be heading toward the government arsenal at Springfield, Massachusetts.

Shays' Rebellion (1786-87)

As the situation worsened, the Congress acted on October 20, 1786. Several states were urged to contribute to a force of 1,340 men to serve for three years. This time, there was no delay by the New England states, but before the complete

Shay's Rebellion began in 1786. It was caused by unfair taxation and cruel evictions. Here is a sample eviction notice.

To the Constables of the Town of Pittsfield in the County of Berkshire, or either of them, greeting.   Whereas it has been represented to us that Elisha Eggleston, his wife and family; John French, his wife and family; Calvin Dunham, his wife and family, - are likely to become burdensome and chargeable to the town if they continue their residence in it, these are therefore to authorize and require you forthwith to warn and notify the above-named persons that they, with their families, immediately depart and remove out of the town, and not to return again, without giving security to the town.

The Massachusetts government called out the militia to crush the rebellion. In their ranks were many Revolutionary War veterans. One of the Lancaster volunteers had served under Captain Daniel Shays during the Revolution. When the militia and volunteers mustered at Worcester, an observer described them:

They are as fine a body of men as were ever assembled, composed of the most respectable characters in the places where they were raised. A circumstance worth relating is: there are in this regiment fifty or sixty persons who have borne commissions, some of which to command regiments in the late continental army and militia, who do duty in the ranks and submit to the hardships attendant on a soldier's life in this inclement season, with a spirit of patriotism and cheerfulness which nothing but the cause they are engaged in could inspire.

In the winter of 1787, General Benjamin Lincoln sent soldiers on sleighs across the countryside to capture the rebels. Learning of success, he recommended that most of the prisoners receive lenient treatment:

To Major-General Paterson
Dear Sir: I congratulate you on our late success. I have no doubt but we shall have it in our power in a short time to disperse the people now in arms
against the Government, and that if the Legislature in their present session shall act with decision and firmness we shall effectually crush the present Rebellion.

If among the insurgents there are any youth or simple men in years, who, from the want of the means of information or from the want of abilities to apply to right objects the information they do receive, such persons I think might be permitted to return to their several homes, after giving up their arms (such men ought not at present to hold them) & taking the oath of allegiance to the Commonwealth.

Those of another Class who have known better than they have acted & are now so convinced of their error, as that their liberation, under bond, may not be dangerous to the well affected, they I think might also be liberated on taking the oaths; There are another class, who, I think should be committed by a warrant from a Justice of the Peace being too inimical to be at large.

I am fully in sentiment with you, that you should not at present, attempt the arresting the most dangerous characters.

Shays has pushed himself into Pelham where he has the strongest ground. I hope however that we shall have it in our power soon to dislodge him: it would be too great a division of our force to detach at present; the earliest opportunity will be embraced for doing it.

You must I think be perfectly secure by keeping your men together as the Insurgents cannot now collect in force without your knowledge & may be taken in detachment.

You may assure all the privates in your division that if they sill surrender themselves, give up their arms & take the oath of allegiance to the State before some Justice of the Peace in your County that they will be recommended to pardon

I have the honor of being Dear Sir with real Esteem
Your obedt. Serv.

B. LINCOLN

force could be raised, the local militia had handled the problem in Massachusetts. This event became known as Shays Rebellion.

Late in January 1787, a portion of the Massachusetts mob led by Daniel Shays attacked the Springfield Arsenal, but was driven back by Massachusetts militiamen. A few days later, a larger force of militiamen from the eastern part of the state arrived in the area and joined with local forces to put down the last remnants of the disorders.

By April 1786, the new force authorized by the Congress had grown by 550 men, whose pay was becoming an embarrassment to a Congress which no longer needed the force. The Congress thus ordered the states to stop recruiting and in fact discharge the men already enlisted, retaining only the two artillery companies required to provide a guard for West Point and Springfield Arsenal. The Massachusetts rebellion is therefore notable for having spurred the first growth in federal forces. It persuaded Americans in general that there was a good case for a stronger central government as the only body that could respond with adequate speed and firmness to any such emergency.

The 1787 Constitutional Convention

These concerns about national security and the nature of the army combined with worries about finance and commercial regulation. The result was a Constitutional Convention that met in the spring of 1787. The main focus of the Convention was the need for a central government with power to regulate military, financial, and commercial affairs. The Convention also concerned itself with how such power could be limited to prevent the central government from becoming too strong. The subject that caused the most concern to the Convention delegates was the military. A general fear about the dangers of a standing army combined with suspicion about the corruptibility,

both moral and physical, of a strong central government. The delegates finally decided after much argument that it was necessary to sacrifice a little freedom for the United States to be safer in the purely military sense. It was decided accordingly that the central government should have considerable military power, but that this power should be checked and balanced by features built into the new Constitution.

The Constitution gave the central government power to raise and maintain an army without making demands on the states. To achieve this military objective, the central government was given the authority to levy taxes to provide the necessary resources. The creation of an entirely new executive branch allowed the day-to-day running of the government without constant reference to the states. However, the exclusive right to declare war, to raise armies, and to create a navy was reserved to the Congress, which also received the right to execute the Laws of the Union, suppress Insurrections and repel Invasions. At the same time, the power of Congress over the militia was limited. While Congress could undertake the organization, equipment, and discipline of the militia and also control "such Part of them as may be employed in the Service of the United States," the states were responsible for the appointment of officers and the training of the militia "according to the discipline prescribed by Congress."

Executive Power to the President

The most important new feature of the Constitution was the giving of all executive power to an elected president. From the military point of view, therefore, the Secretary of War was now responsible not to Congress but to the President, who was named in the Constitution as the Commander-in-Chief of the Army and Navy. In this capacity, the President's powers were very large, but limited "by their nature and by the principles of our institutions." The president could assume command of the forces in the field, but could also delegate this power. The president also became responsible for the use and disposition of the armed forces during peace, and for their overall direction in war.

Perhaps inevitably, the first president was George Washington, who assumed office on April 30, 1789. Congress created the Department of War on August 7 of the same year. In the short term, this was an administrative modification that had little effect on military affairs. Major General Henry Knox remained in charge of the department just as he had headed the army in succession to Washington under the previous system of government. There was no navy as such, so there was no Department of the Navy, and the limited number of naval matters was handled by the Department of War. By now a brigadier general, Harmar was confirmed in his post along with all his officers, so the existing military establishment was taken into the new system in its entirety. At the time that the Department of War came into existence, the United States Army totaled about 800 officers and men. With the exception of the two artillery companies stationed at West Point and Springfield Arsenal, this force was deployed along the Ohio River in a line of forts created after 1785.

Continued Supply Problems

The most important problem faced by the new army was the same one that had plagued the old army, namely supply. The military wisdom of the day said that a quartermaster department was necessary only in war. Therefore, in 1783, the quartermaster general and his staff had been among those discharged from the Con-

Henry Knox
For further references
see pages
6,21,24,25,29

A lithograph of Fort Harmar in 1790 depicts this type of frontier post more idyllically than realistically. It suggests that rural Virginia has been transplanted neatly to the northwest.

tinental Army in favor of a system of civil supply organized by the Secretary of War and funded by the Board of Treasury. This meant that while the Treasury procured and paid for all military supplies, the Secretary of War was responsible for the storage and distribution of these supplies. With the exception of a short time when the Secretary of War was made responsible for food and clothing, the same system was adopted by the new federal government. The one major change was the establishment in 1792 of an Office of the Quartermaster General under civil control for the movement of supplies to frontier posts during the expeditions against the Indians. A more formal organization along the same lines came into being during 1794 with the establishment of the Office of Superintendent of Military Stores within the Department of War, and of the Office of the Purveyor of Public Supplies within the Treasury.

Despite the creation of these new offices, little changed at the practical level of buying and distributing supplies. Contracts were awarded to the lowest civilian bidder for the purchase and delivery of supplies to the men at the contracted military post. Each contractor was obliged to have enough food to feed the troops at all times, and to provide food for at least six months in advance to the more distant posts. Purchase, storage, and transportation of all other supplies were the tasks of a central depot in Philadelphia, where the Superintendent of Military Stores was responsible for issue to the troops as needed. The result of the system was indeed economy, but the food was generally poor and all supplies arrived late.

American Sources of Weapon Procurement

Weapons were supplied through a similar system. As early as 1783, Hamilton had said that the "public manufacture of arms, powder etc." would offer great advantages in terms of guaranteeing the United States independence from foreign deliveries. This sentiment was echoed ten years later by Knox, who told Congress that, while arms could be bought more cheaply in Europe, this was of little importance "compared with the solid advantages which would result from extending and perfecting the means upon which our safety may ultimately depend." Congress was partially convinced by this

A Kentucky pistol of the late 18th century. This flintlock weapon was as distinctive as the Kentucky long rifle. Made in about 1780 by Clark & Son, of London.

argument. The number of American arsenals and magazines was expanded for the storage and supply of more weapons and their ammunition, while national armories were established for the manufacture of weapons. The first national armory was established in 1794 at Springfield, Massachusetts, with a second at Harper's Ferry, Virginia, during the same year. Even so, it was many decades before the United States became independent of European arms supplies.

Control of the Militia Remains in State Hands

The basis on which Washington and Hamilton had argued for the creation of a small standing army was the coexistence of considerably larger militia forces that could boost the numbers of men available in emergencies and wars. The efficiency of these reserve forces would rest on their levels of equipment and training, but Washington and Hamilton were unsuccessful in their efforts to have the militia made subject to federal regulation. In May 1792, Congress passed the basic militia law, which demanded the enrollment of "every able-bodied white citizen" between the ages of 18 and 45 into state companies, battalions, regiments, brigades, and divisions; each militiaman was to be responsible for providing his own weapon, ammunition, and clothing. The result was not the federally controlled militia seen as essential by Washington and Hamilton, but the maintenance of the original militia concept of colonial days with control exercised by the individual states. The importance of the act did not lie in the creation of an effective militia, but in maintaining the American ideal of the citizen-soldier. More important by far in the provisions of the act was the creation of volunteer units to bolster the compulsory system. These volunteer units were formed as companies under elected officers. They trained regularly and formed the basis from which the National Guard was eventually created.

In general, the militia units were not well trained or well disciplined. This was no hindrance to simple military tasks

such as defense in fixed fortifications, but made it very difficult to use the militia as an effective field force. The usefulness of the militia was further reduced by the limits imposed by law on militia tours of duty and the circumstances under which such units could be called into federal service. The militiaman could be called for service in no more than three months in any year, for example, and could not be ordered to serve outside the United States.

The Whiskey Rebellion (1794)

The first occasion on which the president had to call out the militia was the Whiskey Rebellion of 1794. In the western part of Pennsylvania, there had been considerable unrest and resistance to Congressional law since July 1794. Washington responded by sending in a major militia force under Major General Henry Lee. In the face of this armed strength, the unrest faded away without resistance during November of the same year. To this extent, the effort of the militia was completely successful, but Lee's "campaign" failed to provide any indication of the militia's capabilities in a real emergency, civil or military.

In the later 1780s and 1790s, the United States thus found it difficult to create an effective army and its supporting force of militia units. Under these circumstances, the military policy adopted by the United States sensibly took account of four basic factors. First, there was little real threat to the United States. Although Great Britain and Spain wished to prevent the new nation's expansion into their own territories, there was no British wish to reverse the result of the Revolutionary War. Second, the jealous maintenance of states' rights made the creation of a federal army very difficult and defeated all attempts at realistic federal influence on their militia units. Third, the federal government lacked the money to create any more than the framework of an army. Finally, Americans in general were extremely reluctant to serve in the army for more than the briefest time as either a regular or a volunteer. The results were a regular

Officer Ranks in the U.S. Navy (1800-1850)
Midshipman
Sailing Master
Lieutenant
Lieut. Commanding
Master Commandant
Captain
Rear Admiral
Vice Admiral

army that never reached its authorized strength and militia units that were not effective reserves for the regular army.

Trouble in the New Territories

There may have been no external threat to the United States, but in the new territory ceded by Great Britain in 1783, there was plenty of trouble. Settlers were moving into this vast area, larger by far than the original 13 colonies. Their numbers were swelled by ex-soldiers of the Continental Army, who were given grants of land. Both groups wanted government protection against the Indians as well as the establishment of a fair administration. Congress at first thought that a solution could be found in the creation of treaties with the various Indian tribes. But the treaties failed to cope with the problems caused by the large number of settlers and the speed with which they pushed

west. The Indians fought back with bitter courage against the encroachment on their lands, aided by British weapons as well as the presence of the British to the north and west. The scale of the Indian effort is suggested by the death toll in 1787: in that year Indian raids resulted in the killing or seizing of about 1,500 settlers in the Kentucky territory alone.

Sporadic fighting went on along the entire new western frontier, but for a variety of reasons, the government refused to intervene in the southwestern region during the early years of the first presidential administration. The most telling of these reasons was the American treaty of 1790 with the Creeks, the most powerful of the Indian tribes in the southwest. They enjoyed the support of the Spanish in Louisiana, who wished to see no interruption in their profitable trade with the tribe. Direct intervention would have been difficult, because Georgia and South Carolina both made it clear

American problems with the Indians of the southern regions were not as acute as in the northwest. Nevertheless there was trouble, although it was sometimes nipped in the bud by the capture of local chiefs as shown in this illustration.

that they would object to the presence of federal forces in either state.

Army Unpopularity in the Northwest

The northwest was completely different. Here the main task of the army was protection of Indian treaty rights and the expulsion of squatters from public land. Necessary as these tasks were, they made the soldiers unpopular with the settlers and failed to provide the tiny numbers of troops with any realistic training for what was about to happen.

In 1786, the Ohio Company had been formed in Boston to buy from the American government a tract of land for settlement by New Englanders in what is now southeastern Ohio. In 1787, Congress enacted the Northwest Ordinance, a body of law to govern the western lands. Among its provisions were the right of any section of the territory to apply for statehood once its population had reached 60,000 persons, the setting aside of land in every township for the financing of local education, and the outlawing of slavery and involuntary servitude (debt bondage). An indication of the geographical scope of this western movement is provided by three events in one area of present-day Ohio. During April 1788 the first New England settlers began to arrive in the tract of 1,500,000 acres bought by the Ohio Company, traveling down the Ohio River in a clumsy riverboat to the point where the Ohio River is joined by the Muskingum River. Here they soon created the settlement that is present-day Marietta. Later in the same year, a flatboat loaded with New Jersey settlers passed Marietta and reached the mouth of the Little Miami River, where they established Losantiville near Fort Washington (now Cincinnati). In the same year, Virginia claimed a large tract along the Ohio River between the Great Miami and Scioto rivers as the Virginia Military District. It was parcelled out to Virginians who had fought in the Revolutionary War. These early movements soon became a flood of westward migration.

The Maumee War (1790-94)

The Indians were at first happy with their new neighbors, but soon realized that they were being squeezed out. Before long, the first fighting had broken out, and the settlers started to demand federal protection. Implicit in this demand was the threat that if the American government failed them, they would turn for aid to the British or Spanish, striking a severe blow to the unity of the new nation.

The government had not anticipated the problem and was slow to respond. In his first annual message to Congress, Washington demanded the defense of the frontier against the Indians. Congress responded by raising the authorized establishment of the regular army to 1,283 men. As Secretary of War, Knox realized that this force was completely incapable of undertaking what was being asked of it.

Major General Arthur St. Clair, painted by V.Ramage. St. Clair was governor of the Northwest Territory and, after Harmar's defeat in 1790 near the site of present-day Fort Wayne, Indiana, took command of the second expedition against the Maumee people. The Indians inflicted a devastating defeat on the Americans on the upper reaches of the Wabash River. At the time, St. Clair was suffering from asthma, rheumatism, and "colic."

Officer Ranks in the U.S. Marine Corps

Lieutenant
Captain
Major

He called in militia forces to bolster the regular army in their first task: punishing the Indians of the Maumee (or Miami) tribe for their raids against the settlers. Knox emphasized the planned expedition as a potent show of force to deter other Indian tribes from following the same route as the Maumee. Arthur St. Clair, local military commander as well as governor of the Northwest Territory, was appointed co-commander of the expedition with Harmar in June 1790. During the fall of the previous year, St. Clair had been authorized to call on the militias of Kentucky and Pennsylvania if needed, and he now demanded the assembly of 1,500 militiamen at Fort Washington to support Harmar.

Militia Support for the Regulars

As an officer with much experience of the militia's strengths and weaknesses in the Revolutionary War, Knox realized that while this reinforcement for Harmar might not amount to much in the conventional military sense, it offered advantages in fast-moving frontier warfare. Knox accordingly instructed Harmar to use the mounted militiamen as support for the regulars in a "rapid and decisive" expedition to seek out and destroy the Indian tribe and its food supplies. Remote from Knox's personal authority, Harmar and St. Clair instead devised a two-stage campaign completely lacking Knox's fast and decisive movement. Harmar planned a steady advance from Fort Washington north to the Maumee villages near the headwaters of the Wabash River. Under the command of Major John Hamtramck, a second force would advance 150 miles up the Wabash River from Fort Vincennes in present-day Indiana to destroy the Indian villages in this area before linking up with Harmar's force.

Harmar's Defeat

Not surprisingly, given the Indians' knowledge of the country and the American columns' ponderous and highly visible movement, the expedition was a major disaster. Hamtramck left Fort Vincennes on September 30 with the Virginia militia and 330 regulars. Eleven days later, the column had achieved little but the burning of a few villages, and the militiamen refused to move any farther up the Wabash River. Harmar departed from Fort Washington on the same day that Hamtramck left Fort Vincennes. For two weeks, this column of 320 regulars and 1,133 militiamen struggled through the wilderness before reaching the site of the main Maumee settlement near what is today Fort Wayne, Indiana. Harmar paused here, but then, instead of using his complete strength for a decisive attack, on three separate occasions between October 18 and 22, he sent forward detachments of 50 to 60 regulars and between 200 and 500 militiamen each. In each case. the regulars found themselves abandoned as the militiamen took off in search of Indians and booty. Two of these detachments suffered heavy losses in skirmishes with the elusive Indians, and Harmar then returned to Fort Washington after suffering the loss of 200 men. A great deal of criticism was leveled at Harmar, but a court of inquiry cleared the brigadier general on the grounds that he had been forced to use untrained troops and had been compelled to retreat because of the lateness of the season.

The lesson was there to be seen, but was blindly ignored when a second expedition was launched against the Maumee in 1791. The previous year's operations had convinced an unwilling Congress that the regular army was too small, and a second infantry regiment had been added to the authorized establishment. Congress also permitted Washington to enroll a corps of 2,000 men for six months, either from the militia or by enlisting volunteers into federal service. St. Clair was commissioned as a major general and placed in command of the expedition, but recruitment and the building up of supplies proceeded so slowly that it was September 17 before the expedition could depart. As it was, St. Clair could bring his force up to strength only by calling on the militia of neighboring states. The expedition used almost the entire infantry strength of the regular army, some 600 men, supported by 800 enlisted volunteers and 600 militiamen.

The Maumee
For further references
see pages
24,*26*,*29*,*30*,*31*,*34*

Fort Washington
For further references
see pages
14,*24*,*26*,*30*,*32*,*42*,*43*

Arthur St. Clair
For further references
see pages
24,*26*,*29*,*30*,*34*

St. Clair's Defeat

The force moved off from Cincinnati, renamed from Fort Washington at St. Clair's instigation. By November 3, it had covered about 100 miles. On that night, St. Clair camped close to the waters of the Wabash River at a point close to what is today Fort Recovery, Ohio. The Maumee had noted the size of the expedition with alarm; but with considerable skill their chief, Little Turtle, had quickly created a confederation of several tribes. Some of the militiamen had already deserted, and, as the commander had neglected the elementary precaution of scouting the area, the rest of St. Clair's command was then taken completely

by surprise when a force of Maumee, Shawnee, and Delaware Indians attacked just before dawn on November 4. Badly trained, poorly led by an officer suffering from rheumatism and asthma, and inadequately supplied, the Americans were decisively beaten. St. Clair escaped with less than half of his command, with 637 killed and another 263 wounded.

The defeat was a national scandal, and St. Clair resigned in disgrace. So great was the shock of St. Clair's defeat, moreover, that some Americans urged the government to abandon the war and instead take up the British suggestion of an Indian buffer state between the United States and the British possessions in North America. Washington was too

Above: St. Clair's defeat on November 4, 1791, was not the organized occasion suggested by this contemporary illustration, but a rout. The Indians fell on an American force taken completely by surprise; no scouts had been sent out.
Right: The Indian War of 1789-1794, showing the main locations and the sites of important engagements.

THE INDIAN WAR 1789-1794

| 0 | MILES | 30 |
| 0 | KILOMETERS | 48 |

· · · · · · · · · · PRESENT BOUNDARIES

LAKE ERIE

Michigan

Indiana

Battle of
Fallen Timbers   Fort Miami

Fort Deposit

Maumee River

Sandusky River

Harmar's Defeat 1790

St. Joseph River

Fort Defiance
1794

Fort Wayne
1794

Auglaize River

Blanchard's Fork

OHIO

St. Marys River

Upper
Sandusky

Wabash River

Recovery 1793

St. Clair's Defeat 1791

Miami River

Pigeon Town

Scioto River

Piqua

SHAWNEE
SETTLEMENTS

Greenville
1793

Fort Jefferson 1791

Flint lock muzzleloaders were not capable of producing a rapid rate of fire; the process of loading the weapon took too long. First, the powder charge was measured into the barrel and rammed home; then the ball was inserted into the muzzle and rammed home, followed by a wad to hold both powder and ball in position; the weapon was then half-cocked and a needle-like prick was pushed through the vent to make sure that it was clear; finally priming powder was poured into the pan and the weapon was full-cocked; it was now ready to fire.

VIEW OF THE ENCAMPMENT

AND BATTLE GROUND

On the 4th of November, 1791.

A contemporary illustration of the site of St. Clair's defeat on the upper Wabash River, and the disposition of the American forces at the time the Indians fell on them.

clever a political and military leader to be taken in by the superficial attractions of the concept. It would have antagonized the settlers and their supporters in several states and created a power vacuum that would inevitably have led to either or both powers being sucked in, possibly in conflict with each other. Washington therefore ordered the preparation of a third expedition against the Maumee, this time under the leadership of Major General Anthony Wayne. Recalled from retirement after having distinguished himself in the Revolutionary War, Wayne started training his command near Pittsburgh.

New Forces Raised

It was clear that extra forces would have to be found for the new campaign, and Congress effectively doubled the size of the regular army by authorizing three additional regiments, two of infantry and the third as a mixed infantry/light dragoon unit. Short-term enlistment had already shown its limitations, so Congress sought to avoid the problem by

adding the new regiments to the army establishment to be "discharged as soon as the United States shall be at peace with the Indian tribes." At this time, Congress also agreed with Knox's suggestion that the army should be reorganized as a Legion. This name was extensively used in the period to mean a ground formation of the all-arms type. Infantry, cavalry, and artillery components under a single commander were expected to provide the capability for self-sufficient operations. The regular army was thus reorganized as four legions, each commanded by a brigadier general and consisting of two battalions of infantrymen, one battalion of riflemen, one troop of dragoons (cavalry that could fight on their horses or dismounted), and one company of artillery.

Wayne had acquired the nickname "Mad Anthony" in the Revolutionary War, and he was disliked in some circles for his self-centered nature. These characteristics were seldom in evidence as the commander prepared his offensive with a thorough program of training and an insistence that all supplies and equipment be adequate. Wayne demanded tight discipline as he trained his command, and this paid handsome dividends when the carefully planned offensive was committed. In the spring of 1793, Wayne moved his force down the Ohio River to Cincinnati and tried to persuade the Indians to surrender. The offer was refused, and Wayne moved his force 80 miles north to Greenville on the river of the same name. There Wayne completed the preparation of his force during the summer, creating what was almost certainly the best trained force ever to be committed under the American flag. In July, Wayne was bolstered by the arrival of mounted militiamen, and in August, the 3,000-man force set off into the wilderness following St. Clair's route. In its methodical progress, Wayne's force built a series of forts and blockhouses along the line of communication. Despite the training and the commander's clear effort to secure his communications, desertion was still a problem. Morale began to fall before Wayne's command arrived near Fort Miami, recently built by the British on the site of what is now Toledo, Ohio. Here, on the site of present-day Defiance, the Americans caught up with the Maumee main body, which was gathered in a forest clearing created by a storm that had knocked down a number of trees.

The Battle of Fallen Timbers

The fighting on August 20 in the Battle of Fallen Timbers was brutally hard. Almost within range of the guns in the British fort, the Americans held their ground against a determined Indian attack under Little Turtle and, after one hour, counterattacked with the bayonet. The Indians were driven back and then out of the forest so that Wayne's cavalry reserve could launch a planned double encirclement. The result was a complete rout of the Indians at a cost of 33 American dead and another 100 wounded.

Despite the fact that his fort had been built illegally on American soil, the British commander protested about the American action. Wayne ignored the protest and remained in the area to

destroy the Indian villages in the area and to burn the crops before returning to Cincinnati. The Battle of Fallen Timbers broke the spirit of the tribes in this region. In the Treaty of Greenville signed on August 3, 1795, the Indians made peace in an agreement that ceded all their lands in Ohio to the United States. The agreement was made more certain by news that reached them shortly before the treaty negotiations: the British were finally about to abandon their forts on American soil, making continued British support for the Indians improbable.

After the disasters that had befallen the expeditions of Harmar and St. Clair, much rested on the shoulders of Major General Anthony Wayne in the third expedition against the Indians of the northwest. This time, the Americans prepared thoroughly and advanced methodically, and the Battle of Fallen Timbers was a major success that broke the will of the Maumee to resist the settlers any longer.

The Shawnee War (1811)

The suppression of the Maumee and their allies was good news for those waiting to move into the Northwest Territory, and settlers flooded into the region in larger numbers after the Treaty of Greenville. Ohio filled rapidly, which inevitably created pressure on the tribes further west as the flood of settlers showed no sign of ending. In their search for unoccupied farmland, the settlers pushed west past the limits of the territory ceded by

the Maumee in the Treaty of Greenville, into the land of the Shawnees.

In the pattern established by the Maumee under Little Turtle, the Shawnee Chief Tecumseh and his brother, Shawnee Prophet, put together a confederation of Indian tribes throughout the Mississippi Valley to resist the settlers' encroachment into their lands. This alliance received active support from Anglo-Canadian fur interests, which viewed the "domestication" of the Shawnee lands with as much repugnance as the Indians themselves.

During 1800, Congress had divided the

THE OUTER SETTLEMENT LINE 1804

This map of the outer limits of American expansion in 1804 shows how the opening of the Ohio and Cumberland rivers paved the way for development toward the junction of the Missouri and Mississippi rivers.

Right: Generally known as "The Prophet," Tenskwatawac was Tecumseh's brother and another notable Shawnee leader. This painting is by V.Inman.

Northwest Territory into two parts. The western section became the Indiana Territory, and the rest continued as the Northwest Territory. In 1811 the governor of the Indiana Territory was Brigadier General William Henry Harrison. He was urged by the settlers to pre-empt the Indian activities that were becoming inevitable as friction between the settlers and Indians became worse. Harrison agreed that a pre-emptive strike was necessary and devised an operation to defeat the Indians before they could organize any action against the settlers. The operation was approved by the Secretary of War, William Eustis, who added 300 regulars to Harrison's own force of 650 militia, which included a number of mounted riflemen.

Left: Chief Tecumseh of the Shawnee was one of the ablest Indian leaders faced by the Americans in this early phase of the United States' westward expansion.

William Harrison
For further references
see pages
34,40

Women and Children

FALLING VICTIMS TO THE

INDIAN'S TOMAHAWK.

While many of our most populous cities have been visited by that dreadful disease, the Cholera, and to which thousands have fallen victims, the merciless Savages have been as fatally engaged in the work of death on the frontiers; where great numbers (including women and children) have fallen victims to the bloody tomahawk.

Left: An illustration of the period reveals how urban Americans were kept "informed" of conditions and events on the frontier.

Right: A major figure in the history of the northwestern expansion in this period was William Henry Harrison (1773-1841), seen here in an 1812 painting attributed to Rembrandt Peale. Harrison was the victor of the Battle of the Tippecanoe and then an important figure in the War of 1812.

The Battle of the Tippecanoe

Toward the end of September 1811, Harrison led his force north from Vincennes, built a fort on the edge of the Indian lands, and then pushed forward toward "Prophetstown," as the settlers dubbed the main Shawnee village on the Tippecanoe River about 150 miles north of Vincennes. The U.S. force halted on November 6 about a mile from the village on a piece of wooded high ground that commanded the marshy plain surrounding it on all sides. The troops camped in an irregular diamond pattern around the force's wagons. Harrison's situation was not unlike that which led to the defeat of St. Clair in the Maumee War, and it seemed for a time that his

The Shawnee
For further references
see pages
31, 40, 47

Left: The vanguard of American expansion was provided by traders. The Indians initially welcomed the advantages of trade. When they realized that the traders were being followed by settlers, their attitude to the traders frequently altered, a situation encouraged by the British.

Below: The Battle of the Tippecanoe started with a Shawnee attack into the American camp, but the Americans then rallied and drove the Indians back until a virtual stalemate was reached.

Overleaf: The stalemate position in the Battle of the Tippecanoe was broken when mounted riflemen charged the Shawnee position and produced a decisive American victory.

U.S. Army, Light Artillery Regiment, Private, 1808

The Light Artillery Regiment was well equipped and very mobile, with all its men mounted on horses. It was therefore a very valuable support for the infantry, and its men considered themselves an elite force. There was also a militia light artillery company raised by the District of Columbia.

The original of this illustration of Brigadier General William H. Harrison at the Battle of the Tippecanoe carries the caption *"Upon one occasion, as he (General Harrison) was approaching an angle of the Line, against which the Indians were advancing with horrible yells, Lieutenant Emmerson seized the Bridle of his Horse, and earnestly entreated that he would not go there, but the Governor (of the Indian territory), putting spurs to his Horse, pushed on to the point of Attack, where the Enemy were received with firmness and driven back."* Such publicity was instrumental in Harrison's overwhelming success in the 1840 presidential election. Inaugurated in March 1841, Harrison then secured the two unfortunate distinctions of being the first president to die in office, and the president who served for the shortest time.

force would suffer a similar defeat. The Shawnee and their allies attacked just before dawn to start the Battle of the Tippecanoe. The first charge by about 700 men was pressed home with such determination and courage that the Indians penetrated right into the U.S. camp. Although Harrison's force had been taken by surprise, it rallied and then turned the tables on the Indians. The Indians were driven back from the camp, which provided the opportunity for the mounted riflemen to charge and sweep Tecumseh's men from the field.

In the Battle of the Tippecanoe, the U.S. troops suffered 39 dead and 151 wounded, of whom 29 later died. They counted 36 Indian bodies left on the battlefield, but the Indians almost certainly suffered considerably heavier losses, for they carried away a large number of their dead along with the wounded. Harrison then moved on to Prophetstown and burned it, in the short term breaking the power of Tecumseh and causing his tribal federation to dissolve. The problem of white encroachment into Indian lands was not solved, however, so further trouble was sure to follow. The American government realized this, but was faced with renewed war against the United Kingdom, as Great Britain had been renamed on January 1,

A participant in the Battle of the Tippecanoe, Robert McAlee, described the combat in a history he wrote five years later.

The night was dark and cloudy: the moon rose late, and after midnight there was a drizzling rain. Many of the men appeared to be much dissatisfied: they were anxious for battle, and the most ardent regretted that they would have to return without one. The army generally had no expectation of an attack; but those who had experience in Indian affairs suspected some treachery. Colonel Daveiss was heard to say, he had no doubt but that an attack would be made before morning.

It was the constant practice of governor Harrison to call up the troops an hour before day, and keep them under arms till it was light. After 4 o'clock in the morning, the governor, general Wells, colonel Owen, and colonel Daveiss had all risen, and the governor was going to issue his orders for raising the army; when the treacherous Indians had crept up so near the sentries, as to hear them challenge when relieved. They intended to rush upon the sentries and kill them before they could fire: but one of them discovered an Indian creeping towards him in the grass, and fired. This was immediately followed by the Indian yell, and a desperate charge upon the left flank. The guards in that quarter gave way, and abandoned their officer without making any resistance. Capt. Barton's company of regulars and capt. Keiger's company of mounted riflemen, forming the left angle of the rear line, received the first onset. The fire there was excessive; but the troops who had lain on their arms, were immediately prepared to receive, and gallantly resist the furious savage assailants. The manner of the attack was calculated to discourage and terrify the men; yet as soon as they could be formed and posted, they maintained their ground with desperate valor, though but very few of them had ever before been in battle. The fires in the camp were extinguished immediately, as the light they afforded was more serviceable to the Indians than to our men.

As soon as the governor could mount his horse, he proceeded towards the point of attack, and finding the line much weakened there, he ordered two companies from the centre of the rear line to march up and form across the angle in the rear of Barton's and Keiger's companies. General Wells immediately proceeded to the right of his command; and colonel Owen, who was with him, was proceeding directly to the point of attack, when he was shot on his horse near the lines, and thus bravely fell among the first victims of savage perfidy. A heavy fire now commenced all along the left flank, upon the whole of the front and right flank, and on a part of the rear line.

In passing through the camp, towards the left of the front line, the governor met with colonel Daveiss and the dragoons. The colonel informed him that the Indians, concealed behind some trees near the line, were annoying the troops very severely in that quarter; and he requested permission to dislodge them, which was granted. He immediately called on the first division of his cavalry to follow him, but the order was not distinctly heard, and but few of his men charged with him. They had not proceeded far out of the lines, when Daveiss was mortally wounded by several balls and fell. His men stood by him, and repulsed the savages several times, till they succeeded in carrying him into camp.

In the mean time the attack on Spencer's and Warwick's companies on the right, became very severe. Captain Spencer and his lieutenants were all killed, and captain Warwick was mortally wounded. The governor in passing towards that flank, found captain Robb's company near the centre of the camp. They had been driven from their post; or rather, had fallen back without orders. He sent them to the aid of captain Spencer, where they fought very bravely, having seventeen men killed during the battle. The battle was maintained on all sides with desperate valor. The Indians advanced and retreated by a rattling noise made with deer hoofs: they fought with enthusiasm, and seemed determined on victory or death.

As soon as day light appeared, General Wells took command of the corps formed on the left, and with the aid of some dragoons, made a successful charge on the enemy in that direction, driving them into an adjoining swamp through which the cavalry could not pursue them. At the same time Cook's and lieutenant Laribie's companies, with the aid of the riflemen and militia on the right flank, charged on the Indians and put them to flight in that quarter, which terminated the battle.

1801, by an Act of Union.

While the attention of the United States had been focused on the establishment of the new federal government headed by a president, and by the problems on its northwestern frontier, Europe had entered a period of great turmoil. The immediate cause was the French Revolution of 1789, which had led to a general European war. In 1793, Great Britain had joined a European alliance fighting revolutionary France. Immediately, British seapower was applied as its major instrument of strategy. This use of seapower included a blockade of France, and within a year, 300 American merchant ships had been seized. The problem was reduced in 1794 by the signing of Jay's Treaty. The U.S. accepted a British definition of contraband and in return received a firm commitment for the removal of British garrisons in forts on the American side of the frontier with Canada. The treaty played a major part in easing tension between the United States and Great Britain. On the other hand, it antagonized the French and caused distress among many Americans, who were alarmed by this reversal in American policy from its original pro-French and anti-British position.

The United States had a strong desire to remain neutral at a time when the rest of the western world was becoming increasingly polarized for or against France. The ensuing problems were still unresolved when Washington was succeeded as president in 1797 by John Adams. At this time, the authorized strength of the regular army was 3,300

Built in 1790, Fort Washington was one of the bases created in the United States' northwestern expansion. The location of this rural scene is now 3rd Street, east of Broadway, in Cincinnati, Ohio.

John Adams

For further references see pages 59, 89, 91

men, and the all-arms "legionary" establishment that had been successful in frontier fighting was discarded in favor of a return to a traditional military establishment. The army therefore had four regiments of infantry, two companies of light dragoons, and a Corps of Artillerists and Engineers. The shifting nature of the frontier tasks faced by the army in 1796-97 is reflected by a redeployment of the main strength from the northwest to the southwest during these two years. In the northwest, there was a major force of one infantry regiment at Fort Washington, as well as five companies of infantry in Detroit and small garrisons in several frontier forts. In the southwest, nine companies of infantry, the complete dragoon force, and two companies of artillery were stationed. Elsewhere in the United States, small garrisons had been fortified by French experts in a number of ports along the frontier with Canada from the Great Lakes eastward, as well as in older forts such as Carlisle, Fort Pitt, and West Point.

Problems with France and Great Britain

During this period, the main trend of American foreign and military policy was influenced by the country's relations with France and Great Britain. On the larger world stage, therefore, the results were the Quasi-War with France (1798-1800) and the War of 1812 (1812-15). The military establishment evolved considerably during this period.

Soon after Thomas Jefferson became the third president in 1800, France bought a vast territory west of the Mississippi River called Louisiana from Spain. The sale was a blow to the American belief that any weakening of the European presence in North America would automatically lead to the absorption of ex-European possessions into the United States. It also represented a physical problem for the United States for a number of reasons. American policy on the western frontier had until this time been concerned mainly with pacification of the Indians, preventing separatist tendencies by the inhabitants of the western territories, and limiting any friction between American settlers and the Spanish. French ownership of Louisiana opened the possibility of a powerful neighbor to the west. It also led to a restriction on the American practice of sending goods down the Mississippi River for export via New Orleans. Just before the Spanish sold the Louisiana Territory, they cancelled this right, and the French rapidly halted American trade down the river. Another factor that worried the United States was the vast size of the territory, a huge area covering virtually the whole of the modern United States from the Mississippi River westward to the Rocky Mountains with the exception of Texas.

Thomas Jefferson, seen here in a 1788 painting by Trumbull, was the third president and the man responsible for the single largest expansion of the United States through the Louisiana Purchase of 1803. Despite this enormous growth in the United States' land area, Jefferson was also responsible for a reduction in military strength.

The Louisiana Purchase

In 1803, Jefferson offered to purchase Louisiana from the French. To the great surprise of knowledgeable Americans, Napoleon agreed to the sale, because he was faced with the prospect of renewed war in Europe. The Louisiana Purchase, as it is known, added 827,000 square miles to the area of the United States, nearly doubling the size of the nation. Formal possession of Louisiana was taken by the army on December 20, 1803, and small garrisons were soon established in New Orleans and a num-ber of other ex-Spanish posts on the lower reaches of the Mississippi River. The first governor of the territory was Brigadier General James Wilkinson, who had weathered a number of reorganizations to become the army's senior officer.

Even before the Louisiana Purchase, Jefferson had persuaded Congress that an exploration of the continent west of the Mississippi would pay great dividends. The men selected for this extraordinarily important task were a couple of veterans from Wayne's operation in the Northwest Territory, Captain Meriwether Lewis and Lieutenant William Clark. With a party of

Thomas Jefferson
For further references
see pages
43, *45*, 46, 47, 59, 70

Right: Even before the Louisiana Purchase, Jefferson had persuaded Congress of the need for an exploration of the unknown lands west of the Mississippi River, and the acquisition of this vast new territory made the exploration that much more urgent. In May 1804, Jefferson selected his private secretary, Captain Meriwether Lewis, who had served under Wayne against the Indians in the northwest, as joint leader of the expedition.
Below: A contemporary map of the route of the Lewis and Clark expedition between 1804 and 1806.

27 men, Lewis and Clark departed from St. Louis in the spring of 1804, traveled up the Missouri River, crossed the Rocky Mountains, and moved down the Columbia River to reach the coast of the Pacific Ocean near present-day Astoria, Oregon, in November 1805. The expedition returned by a different route, exploring central Montana before marching down the Missouri River to reach St. Louis again in September 1806.

Exploration in the West

Another party sent out by Wilkinson was led by Captain Zebulon M. Pike. Again departing from St. Louis, this 1804 expedition explored the upper reaches of the Mississippi River, reaching a point level with Fort du Lac on the western side of Lake Superior before returning to St. Louis. Pike was sent out from St. Louis once more in 1807. This time, he went west to explore Colorado. Near what is now known as Pike's Peak on the border

The Louisiana Purchase more than doubled the territorial area of the United States. It is worth noting that Lewis and Clark did more than survey a large portion of the new territory. They also pushed beyond it to reach the Pacific Ocean at the mouth of the Columbia River in what is now Oregon.

of the American territory, the 20-man expedition was intercepted by hostile Spaniards, who controlled the land to the west. They escorted the American group south to Santa Fe. The expedition was led by a very circuitous route into Mexico and finally back to American territory at Natchitoches very close to the Red River northwest of New Orleans.

Such incursions into Spanish territory seemed acceptable to most Americans, but they were strongly resented by the Spaniards. During Jefferson's second term of office, the border problem with the Spanish in the west and in the two Floridas became increasingly acute. In 1806, it was reported that Spanish regular troops had been deployed into eastern Texas to bolster the local militia units. Jefferson reacted by calling out the militia forces of the Orleans and Mississippi Territories and sending in about 1,000 regular troops. The report that had spurred this American response proved to be untrue; at no time did the Spanish forces in the area outnumber those of the

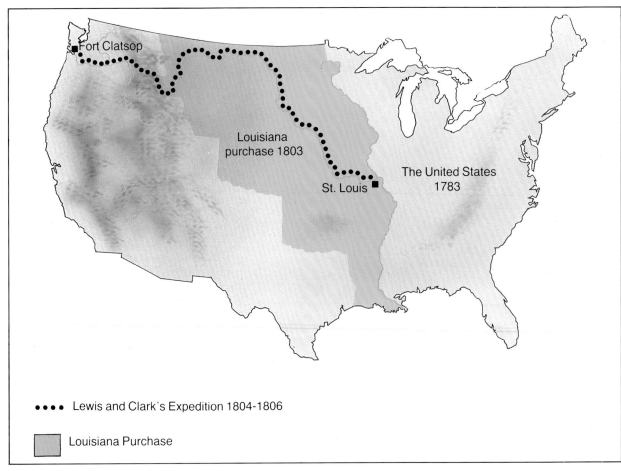

●●●● Lewis and Clark's Expedition 1804-1806

Louisiana Purchase

Americans. The tension of the period is reflected in a number of cavalry skirmishes fought along the Sabine River, but nothing more serious was allowed to happen. The two powers sensibly decided to establish a neutral zone between the Arroyo Hondo and the Sabine River, which became the national frontier up to 1812.

During this period, the political and economic attention of the United States turned increasingly toward Europe. The beginning of the second act of the war between the United Kingdom and France in 1803 was soon to develop into the vast war that ended only with the defeat of Napoleon at the Battle of Waterloo in 1815. The war was fought on an economic as well as military and naval basis, and this trade war involved the United States, which wished to continue its normal pattern of commerce with the fighting powers. This desire led ultimately to the War of 1812.

As the tensions grew, Jefferson finally persuaded Congress that a larger army was essential. In the last month of his administration, Jefferson sent 2,000 men of the regular army to join Wilkinson for the defense of "New Orleans and its

dependencies" against the British invasion that was expected. It did not materialize, but the almost criminal maladministration of the army at this time meant that more than half of Wilkinson's army died in Louisiana. Disease and bad leadership played their part in this dismal tale, but the main burden of guilt must fall on corrupt and inefficient bureaucracy.

The Creek War (1813-14)

Just as Tecumseh and his Shawnees had found the arrival of the white settlers in their lands intolerable, so too the Creeks of the Mississippi Territory found themselves inevitably at loggerheads with American settlement and other influences. The Creeks took a leaf out of Tecumseh's book, and in July 1813 created an alliance with the British, who were at war with the United States at this time.

The Creeks lived in the area of the Continued on page 64

The fur trade created in the territory explored by Lewis and Clark enabled John Jacob to become the richest man in America.

The Creeks

THE BEGINNINGS OF THE U.S. MARINE CORPS

In traditional terms, the role of marines has been that of "shipboard soldiers," sailors with the discipline and weapon skills of the land soldier. Marines were organized in a sea-going corps whose detachments on each warship meant that the ship's officers could retain control of their seamen. They also manned some of the ship's guns and operated on the ship's fighting tops (platforms on the masts) to provide sniper fire into enemy ships in close-range sea battles. Marine detachments also provided a small but useful force that could be landed from ships for small-scale coastal operations.

The first Continental Marine recruits on the Philadelphia waterfront during November 1775. They were soldiers assigned to fight on ships, but not to sail them.

The First Records

The first surviving record of marines in American service dates from May 3, 1775, when Lieutenant James Watson is listed as a marine officer on the payroll of the *Enterprise*, which starts on this date. It is clear, therefore, that marines became a feature, although a small one at first, of the American military effort very early in the Revolutionary War. The word "Marines" was first used by the Continental Congress a few months later, when Major General George Washington of the Continental Army was ordered, on October 5, to secure two armed ships "on Continental risque and pay" and to provide "proper encouragement to the Marines and seamen" for service on these vessels.

Even though American colonial forces and the Continental Army had used marines since the spring of 1775, the birthday of the U.S. Marine Corps is officially November 10, 1775. On this date, the Continental Congress ordered that two battalions of marines should be raised and provided with adequate officers. The senior officer of these "Continental Marines" was Captain Samuel Nicholas, who is therefore reckoned to have been the first Commandant of the U.S. Marine Corps, although the title was not used until 1800. Nicholas received his captain's commission from President John Hancock of the Continental Congress a little more than two weeks later, on November 28. It was, in fact, the first commission issued for service in the Continental Navy and Continental Marines. With the aid of his junior officers, Nicholas set about raising the Continental Marines. By the end of 1775, there were five companies of Continental Marines. Assembled at the Willing and Morris Wharves in Philadelphia, they were allocated to guard duty for Continental warships and stores in Philadelphia. From January 1776, the Continental Marines were deployed on board seven ships of the Continental Navy, starting with the *Alfred*, Commodore Esek Hopkins's flagship.

The First Amphibious Assault

On February 17, 1776, ships of the Continental Navy sailed from Cape Henlopen, Delaware, under the command of Hopkins. Just two weeks later, they made rendezvous off Nassau harbor on the northern side of New Providence in the Bahama Islands, a British possession garrisoned only by small militia forces. The American force made no effort to surprise the British garrison, but when the alarm was raised on the island, the Americans decided to deal first with Fort Montagu, the weaker of the two British forts guarding the island. Just before midday on March 3, Nicholas led a force of 230 Continental Marines and 50 sailors in a landing about two miles east of the fort. This is considered the first amphibious assault by American marines. After his men assembled on the beach after disembarking from their longboats, Nicholas led them against the fort, which they captured in a fight as "bemused as it was bloodless." The U.S. force remained in the fort overnight. On the following day, it moved

Within a month of the Continental Marines' establishment, American marines sailed on the *Alfred*. Their task was to maintain order on the ship and, in battle, to man positions in the fighting tops. Here they could hurl grenades and fire down onto the deck of the enemy ship.

Samuel Nicholas
For further references see pages
50,52,53,62

forward to occupy the rest of the island, taking Fort Nassau and capturing Montfort Browne, the island's governor. That night, the American landing force rested in Fort Nassau, and the fleet patrolled well to the east. This gave the British still at liberty the chance to deprive the Americans of their greatest prize: a sizable quantity of gunpowder was shipped out of the unguarded harbor to St. Augustine, Florida. Hopkins was very angry about the loss, and he stripped the town and the two forts of all their major weapons (about 100 cannon and mortars in all), some powder and ammunition, and a quantity of other military stores. The American force evacuated New Providence on March 17, well satisfied with this first foray by the Continental Marines.

The First Marine Casualties

As the invasion force sailed north, the Continental Marines suffered their first casualty. During the night of April 6, the American squadron met two British ships, HMS *Glasgow* and her tender. On the *Alfred*, the embarked company of Continental Marines was divided into two parties. One was commanded by Nicholas with Second Lieutenant John Fitzpatrick on the main deck, and the other by Nicholas's second-in-command, First Lieutenant Matthew Parke, on the quarterdeck. The first American ship engaged by the *Glasgow* was the *Cabot*. As she fell away under the weight of the British cannon fire, the *Glasgow* turned her attentions to the *Alfred*. In one of the

Above: Accompanied by sailors of the Continental Navy, Continental Marines make the first amphibious landing in American history on New Providence in the Bahamas on March 3, 1776.

first exchanges of fire, Parke was killed by a musket ball, probably fired by a British marine in one of the *Glasgow*'s tops. Nicholas later wrote of Parke that "In him I have lost a worthy officer, sincere friend and companion, that was beloved by all the ship's company." As the fight continued, a shot from the *Glasgow* ripped away the *Alfred's* steering gear. The position for the American flagship was now very difficult, but when the other American ships arrived on the scene, the *Glasgow* made off toward Newport.

On September 5, 1776, a standardized uniform for the Continental Marines (and for the Continental Navy) was adopted by the Marine Committee of the Continental Congress.

The Battle of Lake Champlain

The next battle in which the Continental Marines were involved was defeat for the Americans, but nonetheless provided invaluable time for the American cause at a time of great danger. In the fall of 1776, the British decided to exploit the failure of the American effort against Canada. They planned an advance south up the Richelieu River to Lake Champlain with the objective of taking Saratoga and Albany, and then linking up with the British force in New York. Success would split the rebellious colonies, so that those in New England could be defeated without interference from the middle and southern colonies. The naval battle of Lake Champlain was fought off Valcour Island on October 11, 1776, and resulted in a defeat for the United States under Colonel Benedict Arnold. The survivors of the American squadron managed to slip past the British in the night, but on October 13, the British closed in on the American ships again. Arnold decided that further fighting would result only in useless loss of life and ordered the five remaining galleys to be beached.

Below: Continental Marines raise the American flag over Fort Nassau in the Bahamas on January 27, 1778. This was the first time that the "Stars and Stripes" had been hoisted over a foreign fortification.

Their Continental Marines waded ashore and provided covering fire as the sailors torched the beached vessels.

Changes in Organization

Further organizational change for the marines came on October 30 of the same year, when the Continental Congress resolved that the Continental Marines should have the same titles and ranks (lieutenant, captain, and major) as officers with similar tasks and responsibilities in the Continental Army. The same resolution covered details of how "commanders, officers, seamen, and marines in the continental navy" should be entitled to prizes they took, including privateers. Less favorable to the Continental Marines was an occurrence less than a month later. On November 24, Private Harry Hassen was court-martialed for desertion from the Continental Marines. In this earliest known instance of desertion from the Continental Marines, Hassen pleaded guilty and was sentenced to 50 lashes for desertion and 21 more for "quitting his guard" without being relieved.

The Battle of Princeton

The Continental Marines were also involved in the land war. After his success at Trenton on December 25, 1776, when the Hessian garrison had been completely routed, Washington crossed the Delaware River once more on December 30 and occupied this New Jersey town. Major General Lord Cornwallis, the British commander, responded with an advance from Princeton. Washington sidestepped this

The Continental Marines were involved as ordinary infantry in one of George Washington's most important victories, the Battle of Princeton on January 3, 1777. The American success here, coming hard on the heels of victory in the Battle of Trenton eight days earlier, fanned into flame the embers of a revolution that was dying late in 1776.

British attempt to bring him to battle. On January 3, 1777, he prepared to attack the British base at Princeton. As they got ready to attack, the Americans ran into the last of the British forces marching to reinforce Cornwallis. The British commander, Colonel Charles Mawhood, bombarded the Americans with cannon fire and then sent in a bayonet charge by the 17th Regiment of Foot. The American force under Brigadier General Charles Mercer were pushed back and had to be reinforced by Pennsylvania troops under Brigadier General John Cadwalader and Continental Marines under Nicholas. They, too, were pushed back at first, but Washington arrived and rallied the Americans. The British were defeated.

In 1777, the United States was faced with the loss of Philadelphia, the new national capital. Defensive positions on the Delaware River were built to check any British waterborne approach. The British instead chose an overland approach from Chesapeake Bay. On September 28, Washington realized that the river defenses were being outflanked. He ordered the garrison of Billingsport, on the New Jersey side of the Delaware, to be evacuated to Fort Mifflin, closer to Philadelphia. The land route was closed by the advancing British, so the 112-man garrison of Colonel William Bradford's command had to be taken out by water on October 2, 1777. The task was entrusted to guard boats manned by Continental Marines of the brig *Andrew Doria* under Lieutenants Dennis Leary and William Barney. The marines managed to get out all the men and most of the ammunition; a party remained on shore to spike the American guns and burn the fort. There was a brisk firefight at about midday as the last marines pulled out just as the British arrived.

The Taking of Fort Nassau

At this point, the Bahamas re-enter the history of the Continental Marines. The sloop *Providence*, commanded by Captain John Peck Rathbun, received news in Georgetown, South Carolina, that an old enemy was in Nassau harbor for repairs. It was the British brig *Mary*, which a few months earlier had engaged the *Providence* off New York and caused considerable damage, as well as killing the American ship's sailing master. According to the sloop's captain of marines, Captain John Trevett, "we ware...Determind to Take Fort Nassau and then we Could Have Command of the Town and Harber and take What we Pleased." The American sloop anchored off Hog Island just before midnight on January 27, 1778, and a party of 26 Continental Marines under Trevett was landed one mile west of Fort Nassau. The Americans approached silently, climbed into the fort, and captured the two-man garrison! At dawn, the American flag was raised over the fort, the first time that the "Stars and Stripes" had been hoisted above a foreign possession. The *Mary* and two schooners were captured in the harbor, and a considerable quantity of supplies was seized on shore. On January 30, the captured vessels sailed out to meet the *Providence* for the return journey to New Bedford, Massachusetts.

A Volunteer Company

The Continental Marines also cast their net considerably farther afield in this period. Before the Revolutionary War's beginning, James Willing, a member of an important Philadelphia family, had built up a small trading empire based at Natchez on the lower reaches of the Mississippi River. In the fall of 1777, the influence of his brother was instrumental in securing permission for Willing to create a volunteer company of Continental Marines drawn from the garrison at Fort Pitt, Pennsylvania. This company was then to obtain and arm a large riverboat on the upper reaches of the Ohio River. As it traveled down the Ohio and Mississippi rivers, it would secure the aid (or force the neutrality) of settlers living on the rivers' eastern banks and then return to Fort Pitt with five boats carrying arms and dry goods. Willing and his 34 men departed from Fort Pitt on January 10, 1778, in the armed galley *Rattletrap*. They escaped past the British posts on the river and headed southwest, collecting more men and boats as they went. By the middle of February, Willing's flotilla of boats arrived just north of Natchez, at the plantation of Colonel Anthony Hutchins, a loyalist. By night, Hutchins, his slaves, and many of his possessions were seized and loaded on the *Rattletrap*. A few days later, the expedition reached Natchez, where more loyalists were seized. Then, once he had passed out of the Natchez district, Willing allowed his men far greater freedom of action. What could not be plundered was often burned as the expedition moved south to New Orleans. Here the expedition rested for a time and then launched a series of forays into the loyalist countryside. Willing finally returned to Pennsylvania by sea, while the men of his expedition, commanded by Lieutenant Robert George, headed up the western bank of the Mississippi River with the intention of joining Lieutenant Colonel George Rogers Clark in the Illinois Territory.

John Paul Jones and the *Ranger*

Thousands of miles away, Continental Marines also had their part to play in the activities of Captain John Paul Jones and the *Ranger*. Sailing from the French port of Brest in April 1778, Jones was determined to "end the barbarous ravages perpetuated by the British in America." He wanted to fall on a British coastal town, destroy all ships in its harbor, and seize an important person as a hostage against the release of

Below: Based on a painting by Alonzo Chappel, this engraving shows John Paul Jones, the most celebrated American naval commander of the Revolutionary War. After the Revolutionary War, Jones spent much time in France and then moved to Russia, where he secured a commission as rear admiral in the navy of Empress Catherine the Great. After falling foul of political machinations in Russia, Jones returned to France. He died of pneumonia in Paris during July 1792.

Americans held by the British. The town he selected was Whitehaven, one of the major ports in northwestern England. On April 22, the *Ranger* was too far from the port to attempt anything herself, but Jones, unwilling to lose the advantage of darkness, despatched two boats manned by 30 Continental Marine and seaman volunteers. One boat was commanded by Jones, and the other by a marine officer, Lieutenant Samuel Wallingford. The raid reached Whitehaven but achieved little; the same fate befell his descent onto St. Mary's Isle the next day. A day later, the *Ranger* fell in with a British frigate, HMS *Drake*. The British ship was beaten, but among the three American casualties was Wallingford, who was killed. Jones later commanded the frigate *Bonhomme Richard*, whose marines were volunteers

from a French unit manned by Irish exiles, l'Infanterie Irlandaise, Regiment de Walsh-Serrant. A detachment of this regiment was serving on the *Bonhomme Richard* during the American ship's classic and ultimately successful single-ship action with the British frigate HMS *Serapis* off Flamborough Head on September 23, 1779.

The Assault at Penobscot

The Continental Marines had meanwhile been involved in the largest American amphibious operation of the Revolutionary War, the assault at Penobscot on July 28, 1779. The operation's origins lay with the creation in the spring of 1779 of a strong British outpost at the tip of the

The best known single-ship duel of the Revolutionary War was the September 1779 action between John Paul Jones's *Bonhomme Richard* and HMS *Serapis* off Flamborough Head or the east coast of England. Both ships were reduced to virtual wrecks before the *Serapis* struck her colors to the American ship; the *Bonhomme Richard* sank two days later.

BON HOMME RICHARD & SERAPIS

Bagaduce peninsula in Penobscot Bay, lying in the northern part of Massachusetts which is now Maine. Fort George was constructed and garrisoned by 700 men of the British 74th and 82nd Regiments of Foot under Brigadier General Francis McLean, military governor of Nova Scotia. The Americans decided to evict the British, and 3,000 militia troops assembled in Boston under Brigadier General Solomon Lovell. Meanwhile, Captain Dudley Saltonstall of the *Warren* coordinated a naval force of six Continental and Massachusetts state ships, bolstered by 13 privateers as escort for 20 troop transports. The American expedition sailed on July 19, 1779, and arrived in Penobscot Bay on July 26. Two days later, a force of 200 Continental Marines and 20 militiamen under Captain Walsh landed under the bluff on the peninsula's western approaches. With the marines to the fore, the American force took the bluff, but then failed to make much more progress. Two weeks later, a large British naval force appeared, and the American ships retreated up the Penobscot River. There the ships were burned, and the Americans retreated southwest through the wilderness of Maine. British losses included 13 killed, while those of the Americans amounted to 474 dead and many others wounded. Saltonstall was court-martialed and dismissed from the service.

The Continental Marines continued to find action, most notably on the ships of the Continental Navy. Typical is the action fought on May 29, 1781, between the frigate *Alliance*, under Captain John Barry, and two British sloops, HMS *Atalanta* and HMS *Trepassey*. The *Alliance* was returning from France and, between the Newfoundland Banks and the American coast, was engaged by the two smaller

The landing at the mouth of the Penobscot River on July 19, 1779, was the largest American amphibious operation of the Revolutionary War. The resulting operation was a complete disaster: it cost the Americans 474 lives, but the British lost only 13 dead.

ships on a virtually windless day. Visibility was soon reduced to zero by the cloud of gunpowder smoke that enveloped the scene, and the Continental Marine marksmen in the tops of the American frigate found it very difficult to find any targets. In mid-afternoon, the wind returned, and the *Alliance* devastated the *Trepassey* with a short-range broadside before meting out similar punishment to the *Atalanta*. Both British ships struck their colors.

On the other side of the United States, George Rogers Clark (now a brigadier general) was faced with the important but immensely difficult job of maintaining American control over the valley of the Ohio River. Particular emphasis was placed on command of the area between the mouths of the Miami River and Licking Creek, and Clark decided that an armed galley offered his limited manpower the best chance of achieving this task. Powered by 46 oars or - when the wind was favorable - the sails on two masts, the *Miami* had a 73-foot keel and was armed with eight cannon. The vessel was completed late in May 1782 and was manned by 110 men, including the gun crews provided by a company of Virginia State Marines under Captain Jacob Pyeatt. The vessel was effective in its planned role: the Shawnee Indians were so concerned that they abandoned a plan to raid Wheeling to concentrate their efforts on the invasion they thought was imminent. The vessel was sunk in September 1782, and the marines were transferred to the Illinois Regiment for the rest of the Revolutionary War.

The End of the Revolutionary War

News of the end of the Revolutionary War reached the *Alliance*, the last frigate of the Continental Navy on active service, on March 31, 1783, as she lay off Petuxet about five miles from Providence, Rhode Island. The ship was now marked for use as a cargo vessel, and the crew was paid off on April 1. Included in the total were 33 of the last 41 men remaining in the Continental Marines. The last

man, Lieutenant Thomas Elwood, was discharged about six months later, and the seven-year history of the Continental Marines came to an end. It is thought that 131 officers held commissions in the Continental Marines, and that about another 2,000 men served as non-commissioned officers and enlisted men. Of this total, 49 had been killed in battle or died of their wounds, while another 70 had been wounded but recovered. This compares with 4,044 dead and 6,004 wounded in the army, and 342 dead and 114 wounded in the navy.

The need for marines was appreciated again in the Quasi-War with France. On July 11, 1798, President John Adams approved an act introduced to the Congress by Samuel Sewall, chairman of the House Naval Committee. The act provided for a Marine Corps of 33 officers and 848 "non-commissioned officers, musicians and privates," and Major William Ward Burrows was appointed the major commandant.

The Creation of the Marine Band

After the creation of the new Marine Corps, developments occurred quite rapidly. Some were small matters in themselves, but through custom and tradition, they enjoy greater significance. Typical was the creation on July 11, 1798, of the Marine Corps Band. Known as "The President's Own," it has the double distinction of being the oldest American military band and the only musical organization with the principal task of providing music for the president. The band played at the first New Year's Day reception at the president's new residence in Washington, D.C. Because of the limited space in the Oval Office, only six musicians could be used in this first important social event held in the president's official home. On July 4 of the same year, President Thomas Jefferson reviewed the Marine Corps, led by the Marine Corps Band, in the grounds of the White House. It was the first occasion on which a body of regular troops had been reviewed by the

The capture of the British brig *Reindeer* by the American sloop *Wasp* during the War of 1812 took only 29 minutes. In the action, the Marines on board the *Wasp* played a skillful and major part.

president in his role as commander-in-chief, at his official residence.

By this time, the Quasi-War with France had been ended, but during this strange conflict, the new Marine Corps was blooded, principally in the detachments it provided for American warships. In the first half of 1800, the corps undertook its first amphibious operation, however, and thereby paved the way for the type of martial activity that was to become its main military task. Commodore Silas Talbot was cruising in the frigate *Constitution* north of the Spanish possession of Santo Domingo (now the Dominican Republic) on the eastern end of the island of Hispaniola. He learned that a French privateer was lying at Puerto Plata, protected by Spanish guns. The privateer had been the *Sandwich*, a British packet thought to have a valuable cargo on board. Talbot knew that the *Constitution* had too deep a draft for his scheme of cutting out the privateer, so he impressed the sloop *Sally*. This task was entrusted to Lieutenant Isaac Hull, whose sailors were reinforced by a detachment of the *Constitution's* marines under Captain Daniel Carmick. The *Sally* sailed into Puerto Plata during May 12 in broad daylight. The French privateer was protected not only by her own guns, but by a battery of Spanish artillery as well. Despite this fact, Hull took the *Sally* alongside the French ship and used his sailors to take her without losing a man. As this was being completed, Carmick and his marines landed, took the Spanish battery and spiked its guns, and then pulled back to the captured ship before the Spanish could send in reinforcements. In the absence of any wind, the Americans were forced to wait until the following morning to leave Puerto Plata with the *Sally* and their prize.

The War of 1812

The Marine Corps next saw land action on the shores of Tripoli later in the same decade. The corps was also involved in the War of 1812, losing a total of 45 men killed and 66 wounded. Most of the

Marine Corps activities were connected with the war at sea, but there was also a fascinating episode in the Marquesas Islands of the South Pacific. The frigate *Essex*, under Captain David Porter, was cruising in search of British whalers and other merchantmen. On May 30, 1813, one of the *Essex*'s prizes, the *Greenwich*, was entrusted to a Marine Corps officer, First Lieutenant John M.Gamble. He commanded the vessel in action against HMS *Seringapatam*, the first occasion on which a Marine Corps officer had commanded an American "naval" vessel in action. Toward the end of 1813, Porter concentrated his frigate and her prizes at the island of Nuku Hiva in the Marquesas. Intending to make a short cruise in the area, Porter left the prizes *Greenwich*, *Seringapatam*, and *Sir Andrew Hammond* under the command of Gamble. After building a small fort, he departed from the island during December, leaving a garrison of Gamble, one midshipman, and about 20 marines and sailors.

After the *Essex*'s departure, the is-

Lieutenant Stephen Decatur and his party of sailors and Marines board the captured *Philadelphia* in Tripoli harbor before burning the ship.

landers became hostile to the Americans. The local leader, Chief Gattenewa could not prevent a spate of thefts from the fort, and Gamble had to make a show of force before the islanders handed back the stolen goods and stopped creating problems. The situation lasted until May of the following year.

By this time, Gamble realized that Porter was not returning. During April, he ordered his force to start preparing the *Seringapatam* and *Sir Andrew Hammond* for the journey to Valparaiso, Chile the emergency rendezvous agreed with Porter. On May 7, however, the crew of the *Seringapatam* mutinied. Gamble was wounded, and the ship sailed from Nuku Hiva. Two days later, the islanders, realizing how weak the force now was, attacked the fort. The midshipman and three men were killed, and one of the marines was seriously wounded. This left Gamble with just three marines and three sailors for the *Sir Andrew Hammond*, and of the six men, only two were fully fit. The *Greenwich* was burned, and the *Sir Andrew Hammond* sailed on May 9. On the last day of the month, Gamble reached the Yahoo Islands and, securing a crew of islanders, sailed again on June 11. Only two days later, however, the American prize was captured by the British ship *Cherub*. Arriving in the Brazilian port of Rio de Janeiro, the British freed the Americans. The following year, Gamble managed to secure passage on a Swedish ship destined for Havre de Grace in France, but managed to transfer to an American ship, the *Oliver Ellsworth*, at sea. He finally reached New York in August 1815.

Marines at Puerto Rico

In 1824, the Marine Corps was involved in an extraordinary event. An American trading house on St. Thomas in the Virgin Islands had been robbed and the stolen goods shipped to the small port of Fajardo on Puerto Rico, then a Spanish possession. In October, news of these reached Lieutenant C.T. Platt of the *Beagle* who agreed to help recover the

Commandants of the U.S. Marine Corps	
Samuel Nicholas	1775 - 1781
William Ward Burrows	1798 - 1804
Franklin Wharton	1804 - 1818
Anthony Gale	1819 - 1820
Archibald Henderson	1820 - 1859
John Harns	1859 - 1864
Jacob Zeilin	1864 - 1876
Charles G. McCawley	1876 - 1891
Charles Heywood	1891 - 1903
George F. Elliott	1903 - 1910
William P. Biddle	1911 - 1914
George Barnett	1914 - 1920
John A. Lejeune	1920 - 1929
Wendell C. Neville	1929 - 1930
Ben H. Fuller	1930 - 1934
John H. Russell	1934 - 1936
Thomas Holcomb	1936 - 1943
Alexander A. Vandegrift	1944 - 1947
Clifton B. Cates	1948 - 1951
Lemuel C. Shepherd, Jr.	1952 - 1955
Randolph McC. Pate	1956 - 1959
David M. Shoup	1960 - 1963
Wallace M. Greene, Jr.	1964 - 1967
Leonard F. Chapman, Jr.	1968 - 1971
Robert E. Cushman, Jr.	1972 - 1975
Louis H. Wilson	1975 - 1979
Robert H. Barrow	1979 - 1983
Paul X. Kelly	1983 - 1987
Alfred M. Gray, Jr.	1987 -

goods. Platt arrived in Fajardo on October 26 and, accompanied by Lieutenant Ritchie, called on the Spanish authorities. They promptly arrested the two officers as pirates, even though Platt produced his U.S. Navy commission. Finally, the Americans were allowed to return to the *Beagle*, and they departed. Soon though, the *Beagle* met the *John Adams*, whose Commodore John Porter decided that the Puerto Rican insult to the Americans must be punished.

The *John Adams* drew too much water to berth in Fajardo, so Porter embarked a party of his ship in boats and, escorted by the *Beagle* and the *Grampus*, entered Fajardo harbor. As the ships were about to anchor, it became clear that a shore battery was about to fire on them. A party of 14 marines under Lieutenant Thomas B. Barton, a passenger on the *Grampus*, was landed to spike the guns, which they did without difficulty. On November 14, Porter landed with about 200 marines and sailors, and sent forward a naval officer with a letter to the governor demanding apologies and restitution. These demands were met, and Porter's party returned to their ships. This was not the end of the matter, however, for the American authorities deemed that Porter had overstepped his authority. The naval officer was court-martialed, found guilty, and sentenced to a six-month suspension. Porter resigned, however, and later accepted a commission as commander-in-chief of the Mexican navy.

U.S. Marines Land in the Falkland Islands

In 1832, there was a marine landing in the Falkland Islands, at that time under Argentine control. In this period, the islands were the center of a considerable international trade in seals. In 1831, the American schooners *Breakwater*, *Harriet*, and *Superior* had been seized on the order of the islands' governor. Confusion about the sovereignty of the Falklands in the period is evident in President Andrew Jackson's annual report to Congress that year. He mentioned "a band acting, as they pretend, under the authority of the Government of Buenos Ayres" and suggested measures "for providing a force adequate to the complete protection of our fellow-citizens fishing and trading in those seas." Congress approved the president's plan, and the sloop *Lexington*, under Commander Silas Duncan, was ordered from Buenos Aires to handle the matter. The *Lexington* arrived in Berkeley Sound, East Falkland, on December 28, 1831, before sailing into the anchorage of St. Louis on January 1, 1832. Duncan sent ashore a party of two officers and 15 men (presumably

marines) in a commandeered schooner. More marines and sailors followed in two boats later in the same morning. This was pressure enough to secure the release of the three arrested schooners. Virtually every American on the islands wanted to leave, and Duncan agreed to transport these refugees to Montevideo. Landing parties of marines patrolled the property of the Americans until the expedition set sail on January 22.

Early Landings

The early history of the Marine Corps is filled with such episodes. Landings were undertaken in 1832 on Sumatra; in 1833 in Argentina; in 1835 and 1836 in Peru; in 1838 and 1839 in Sumatra; in 1840 on the Fiji Islands; in 1841 on Drummonds Island and Samoa; in 1843 at points on the West African coast; in 1851 on Johanna Island; in 1852 in Argentina and Nicaragua; in 1853 in Japan, the Luchu (now Ryukyu) Islands, Nicaragua and Siam (now Thailand); in 1854 in China, Japan, the Luchu Islands, and Nicaragua; in 1855 in China, the Fiji Islands, and Nicaragua; in 1856 in China; in 1858 on the Fiji Islands and Uruguay; in 1859 in China; and in 1860 in Africa, Colombia, and Japan. All were small actions, usually in support of civil authorities or to rescue American citizens and interests, and frequently accomplished without bloodshed through a show of force.

It is also worth noting that on June 30, 1834, Congress passed a bill "For the Better Organization of the Marine Corps." The corps was established as part of the navy, its strength was increased, and its commandant, Archibald Henderson, was promoted to colonel. Henderson soon departed to fight in the Second Seminole War, leaving tacked on his door a note that read: "Have gone to Florida to fight Indians. Will be back when the war is over." Elements of the Marine Corps served in Florida until 1838, but in recognition of his services, Henderson was brevetted a brigadier general, the Marine Corps' first general officer, on January 27, 1836.

Born in March 1757 in Waxhaw Settlement, South Carolina, Andrew Jackson was a self-taught lawyer who saw the military as a way of publicizing his name and advancing his career. Jackson was also enthusiastic about the concept of a larger United States, and saw the opening of a southern theater during the War of 1812 as a heaven-sent opportunity for both the United States and himself.

Continued from page 47

Mississippi Territory that later became Alabama. In the summer of 1813, they took the offensive in a series of increasingly severe attacks that culminated in the overrunning of Fort Mims on August 30. The fort lay about 35 miles up the Alabama River from Mobile on the American side of the frontier with the western half of Spanish West Florida, which had recently been occupied by the Americans. Garrisoned by 550 militiamen, it had been swelled in population by the arrival of large numbers of civilians fleeing the rampaging Indians. More than half

of those in the fort, numbering about 500, were massacred by the Indians.

At Natchez on the Mississippi River, a force of 2,000 Tennessee militiamen had been entrusted by the state to the command of Major General Andrew Jackson. He proposed an invasion of both Floridas as part of the War of 1812. The American government preferred a less ambitious scheme by regular forces under Wilkinson, and the Tennessee army was at Natchez awaiting return home. From this state militia, Jackson quickly created a volunteer force that advanced into

Andrew Jackson
For further references see pages
65,67,70,78,79,80,82, 87,107,120

A map of Andrew Jackson's Indian and Gulf campaigns between 1813 and 1815.

the Mississippi Territory. A military commander notable for his enthusiasm rather than his concern with such essentials as adequate supplies and a safe line of communications, Jackson swept on so impetuously that he had soon moved beyond the limits of his minimal supply system and was forced to live off the land. Jackson's force nonetheless managed to inflict tactical reverses on the Creeks at Tallasahatchee on November 3 and at Talladega on November 9. The militia force was then itself defeated. As the men were already discouraged by their lack of supplies, Jackson decided to await supplies and reinforcements at Fort Strother on the upper reaches of the Coosa River. In this entrenched position, the increasingly mutinous Tennessee militia wintered, and only the arrival of an infantry regiment of the regular army in February 1814 made it possible for Jackson to restore order within his own command and plan further offensive action against the Indians. The Creeks meanwhile had recovered from their defeats of the previous year and now posed as great a threat as before.

The Battle of Horseshoe Bend

In March, Jackson felt that he was ready. He moved his command against the main Creek force of about 900 men; together with large numbers of women and children, gathered in the Horseshoe Bend area of the Tallapoosa River. Jackson's force was made up of about 2,000 militia and volunteers supported by just under 600 regulars, several hundred friendly Indians, and a few pieces of artillery. Jackson's force fell on the Creeks in the Battle of Horseshoe Bend on March 29. The main part was played by the regulars, who completely routed the Creek warriors with a firm bayonet charge. The rest of the force was launched in a ruthless pursuit of the Creeks as they fled toward Spanish territory, which only 100 warriors reached. American casualties were 201, and a few Creek noncombatants were

also killed. Jackson himself said: "I lament that two or three women and children were killed by accident."

The war was ended by the Treaty of Fort Jackson on August 9, 1814. In overall terms, the Creek War had been of little significance, even within the context of the War of 1812. On May 22, Jackson had been rewarded for his success by a commission as major general in the regular army and was placed in command of the Gulf coast region.

The Treaty of Ghent

On February 13, 1815, news arrived in Washington, the new capital of the United States, that the War of 1812 had been ended by the Treaty of Ghent, signed on December 24, 1814. There followed a period in American military history often called "The Thirty Years' Peace." This period was certainly free of any type of warfare against foreign enemies, but it did

Left: Another man destined for greater things was Samuel Houston. At the time of the Creek War, young Houston was a second lieutenant. In the Battle of Horseshoe Bend he showed considerable courage when he was hit in the leg by an arrow.
Right: James Monroe, in a painting attributed to Herring. A protege of Thomas Jefferson, who taught him law and persuaded him to enter political life, Monroe was Secretary of State and then Secretary of War in the administration of President James Madison. Capitalizing on his considerable success in these two offices, Monroe won the 1816 presidential election and was inaugurated as the fifth president in March 1817.

U.S. Regular Army, Staff Officer, c1810

The military staffs of the period were very small by comparison with those of modern armies. Even so, the staff officer of the period had a distinctive uniform. In action, only the aide-de- camp (senior officer's assistant) was allowed to wear the crimson sash worn by all other army officers.

Throughout this period, there was continual skirmishing along the frontiers of the settled region. This striking image depicts an episode in the frontier fighting during 1812, when Daniel Boone and two companions were attacked by Indians, who killed and scalped John Stewart as the other two Americans escaped.

Washington
For further references see pages 59, 67, 70, 78, 100, 108, 111

contain a number of frontier conflicts with various Indian tribes.

At the time, though, the prospect of sustained peace seemed unlikely. In Europe, it was generally assumed that the United Kingdom, having with its allies completely eliminated any armed threat from France, would soon turn its attentions to the re-conquest of the lost part of its American empire. This feeling was gloomily reported to the Secretary of State, James Monroe, by Brigadier General Winfield Scott, who was in Europe during the summer of 1815. Scott was impressed with the quality of the allied armies that had finally brought defeat to Napoleon, one of history's greatest captains. The American general was also devoting considerable effort to a tactical study of the Napoleonic Wars, and to collecting all current British and French studies on army organization and training. Professional soldiers in the United States argued about the tactical and operational implications of the Napoleonic Wars, and about whether there was still validity in the concept of total war as embodied in the phrase "the nation in arms." Intertwined with these thoughts about warfare as fought between the major European powers was

consideration of the performance of the U.S. forces in the War of 1812. The consensus of professional soldiers was that the day of the militiaman was effectively over. All agreed that militia forces had undoubtedly contributed to American success in several battles, but the professionals were increasingly concerned about organizing an effective army and laying sensible plans when it was difficult to obtain from the states any accurate figures of how many militiamen they each possessed, and how each militia unit was armed, organized, disciplined, and trained.

Army Cut-backs

Almost immediately after the end of the War of 1812 had been announced publicly by President James Madison, Congress met to consider the future of the American army. The session was held at Blodgett's Hotel in Washington because the Capitol was in ruins after its destruction by the British in August 1814. This reminder of the nation's vulnerability clearly played its part in the decision of Congress to create a larger but more

69

efficient regular army that would form the major defense of the United States in collaboration with the state militias. The authorized strength was set at 10,000 men excluding the Corps of Engineers, a figure only about one-third of the army's peak strength in the War of 1812, but more than three times that of the 3,220-man establishment under Jefferson. Congress was determined that the army should be not only larger, but also considerably more efficient in terms of organization and leadership. The organization, created during the War of 1812, of nine military districts (headed mainly by elderly officers who had distinguished themselves in the Revolutionary War) was replaced by a more streamlined arrangement of two divisions. The Division of the North had four territorial departments and was headed by Major General Jacob Brown, while the Division of the South had five territorial departments and was headed by Major General Andrew Jackson. Both commanders had distinguished themselves in the War of 1812 and were expected to breathe new life into their commands.

At the head of this organization was a new Secretary of War, the first full-time holder of the office for more than 12 months. In August 1814, public opinion had reacted to a series of misfortunes, culminating in the British occupation of Washington, by forcing the resignation of John Armstrong. Over the next few months, Secretary of State Monroe had also acted as Secretary of War until the spring of 1815, when illness forced him to hand over the Department of War to Secretary of the Treasury Alexander Dallas. Then, President Madison appointed William H. Crawford, the U.S. Ambassador to France, as the new Secretary of War, and Crawford arrived back from Europe in August 1815 to take up his new position.

The new secretary had previously been a distinguished Senator and had refused the position of Secretary of War that had then been accepted by the unfortunate Armstrong. Despite his later assignment to France, Crawford had maintained a deep interest in the U.S. Army, particularly in the General Staff established by Congress in the spring of 1813.

It was not a general staff in the modern sense, covering the full spectrum of operational concerns, but an organization to oversee the army's "housekeeping functions." For this reason, therefore, the General staff controlled the Adjutant General's, Hospital, Inspector General's, Ordnance, Pay, Purchasing, Quartermaster's, and Topographical Departments, together with the Judge Advocates, the Chaplains, and the Military Academy. It also had authority over commanding generals of the nine military districts and their logistical staffs. Congress also decided that certain officers from this organization (most notably the Adjutant and Inspector General plus two assistants, the Commissary General of Ordnance plus three assistants, the Paymaster of the Army, and the Assistant Topographical Engineer) should be based in Washington to provide the Secretary of War with a small but professional staff in place of his previous "staff" of just a few clerks. As early as 1813, Crawford had urged from France that "For God's sake," it was essential to "endeavor to rid the army of old women and blockheads, at least on the general staff."

Crawford as Secretary of War

In fact, it was the reorganization in the spring of 1915 that finally removed those to whom Crawford rightly objected. Crawford urged Congress to maintain the General Staff as part of the peacetime establishment. The course of the War of 1812's early campaigns had convinced him of "the necessity of giving to the military establishment, in time of peace, the organization which it must have to render it efficient in a state of war." Crawford's understanding was extremely far-sighted. The only major modification wanted by the new Secretary of War was the addition of the Quartermaster General to those officers allocated permanently to the management staff in Washington, plus an increase in the size of the Corps of Engineers. Congress accepted Crawford's proposals on April 24, 1816, and only a few days later authorized the President to secure the

Continued on page 74

This map shows the military posts in the western United States in the period from 1815 to 1825, together with the boundary between the army's Eastern and Western Departments in 1821.

Fort Brady

Fort Holmes

Fort Snelliman

Fort Howard

Fort Saginaw

Fort Crawford

Fort Gratiot

Fort Shelby

Fort Dearborn

Fort Atkinson

Fort Armstrong

Engineers Cantonment

Fort Wayne

Fort Clark

Fort Edwards

Fort Harrison

Fort Osage

Newport

Belle Fontaine

Fort Gibson

Fort Smith

Fort Hampton

Fort Deposit

Fort Towson

Fort Strother

Fort Williams

Augusta

Fort Hawkins

Fort Jackson

Cantonment Montpelier

Fort Mitchell

Fort Claiborne

Camp Montgomery

Camp Ripley

Fort Selden

Fort Crawford

Trader's Hill

Fort Jessup

Fort Stoddart

Baton Rouge

Fort Charlotte

Fort Barrancas

Pass Christian

Fort Gadsen

New Orleans

Cantonment Clinch

Fort St. Philip

Fort Jackson

Cantonment Brooke

Military Posts in the United States, 1815 - 1825

Division between Eastern and Western Departments, 1821

Early American Firearms

Very little is known of the firearms of the earliest colonists, though it is clear that they used the matchlock type of weapon. The match, a short length of hemp cord impregnated with saltpeter and other chemicals to make it burn steadily at between three and five inches an hour, was held in the screw-adjusted jaws of the lock's cocking piece. When the firer pulled the trigger, a spring turned the cocking piece so that the lighted tip of the match plunged down into a pan filled with priming powder, whose ignition flashed down a vent (the touchhole) into the barrel and set off the main charge of powder behind the bullet.

The Wheel Lock

The next development in weapon technology was the wheel lock, which offered a considerably higher chance of successful ignition. It worked on the same principal as the modern cigarette lighter: when the trigger mechanism was activated, a serrated steel wheel was spun by a coil spring that had to be wound with a special key. It struck a flint to produce a shower of sparks that ignited the powder in the priming pan. The wheel lock mechanism was expensive to make and difficult to maintain, so it never became common on the weapons of the American colonists.

Further development produced the snaphaunce, which was based on the tinder lock, an improved version of the matchlock. In the snaphaunce, the adjustable jaws of the cocking piece held a piece of pyrites. It was driven by the spring of the mechanism against a steel anvil beside the priming pan, creating the sparks needed to ignite the powder. The Massachusetts Bay Company imported snaphaunce weapons for its paid troops in 1628. The final development of this weapon was the flintlock, which was basically the snaphaunce with a lid over the priming pan to stop the powder from getting wet or blowing away. As the cocking piece descended, it struck the hinged cover and threw it back to expose the powder.

The Need for Firearms

From the beginning of the American colonies, the settlers had to hunt, and in due course they came increasingly into conflict with the Indian tribes of the eastern seaboard. They needed effective firearms, and although the records are scanty, it is inevitable that weapons were first imported, and facilities for maintenance and then manufacture were established in the colonies. The earliest settlers were British and so came from stock that was not notable for its interest or skill in the manufacture of firearms.

The arrival of German and Swiss settlers changed things. Many of the new settlers came from stock historically involved in the development and manufacture of firearms. The Germans settled mainly in Pennsylvania, and soon began to develop a truly American type of weapon. The heritage of the new gunsmiths was European, which emphasized heavy weapons with a large bore (internal diameter of the barrel). In Pennsylvania, the gunsmiths swiftly realized that modifications to this pattern were essential. Barrels up to 48 inches long were introduced for better combustion of the main powder charge, and as this also permitted the installation of the sights on a longer base, accuracy was improved to a very considerable degree. Despite the increased weight of the extended barrel, overall weight remained basically the same, gunsmiths re-designed the wooden stock (made mainly of American maple or walnut) to eliminate all sections that were not strictly necessary. Even so, the length of the stocks was gradually increased to protect much of the barrel, which might otherwise have been damaged in the thick forests.

American Gunsmiths

By 1700, small gunsmithing businesses were producing excellent and characteristically American weapons, and by 1732 men such as the Heinrich brothers and Peter Leman

"Trade from the Monongahela" by Gayle Hoskins reveals aspects of rifle manufacture, repair, and maintenance.

were producing weapons acknowledged to be as good as any in the world. The finest of these weapons were rifled types with sophisticated sights, capable of considerable accuracy over a long range. The early weapons had an average caliber of .54 inch and fired a ball weighing about half an ounce, but these figures were soon reduced in the interests of accuracy and range. Rate of fire, was improved considerably by a completely American revision to the art of loading the rifle. European loading meant that a slightly oversized bullet was started down the barrel by being hammered into the muzzle before being punched down onto the powder charge with the ramrod. The new American system used a slightly undersized bullet wrapped in linen or buckskin that had been soaked in tallow. This not only improved speed of loading, but also provided a better seal between the bullet and the barrel, reducing the loss of propellant gas when the rifle was fired and therefore improving range and accuracy.

These American weapons were made mainly in Pennsylvania but were called Kentucky rifles, because they were used mainly in the region then called Kentucky, lying between the Cumberlands and the Mississippi River. The Kentucky rifle's accuracy has been greatly exaggerated in stories over the years, but it was nevertheless the greatest precision firearm of its day.

The Demands of War

With the outbreak of the Revolutionary War in 1775, there was an urgent demand for military weapons, all flintlocks and mainly of the smooth-bore musket type. Procurement resulted from the recommendation of the Committee of Safety, and flintlock weapons were made by more than 200 gunsmiths in Maryland, Massachusetts, Pennsylvania and Rhode Island. These weapons weighed about ten pounds each and had calibers ranging from .72 to .80 inch. French support for the American cause resulted in substantial deliveries of weapons and the Americans received

large numbers of the Charleville musket, notably the Model 1763.

With the flintlock, the firearm had reached a plateau as a weapon using mechanical means for ignition. The next step was the adoption of chemical means in the percussion lock. In its first practical form, developed early in the 19th century, the percussion lock was a simple adaptation of the flintlock in which the cocking piece, now ending in a hammerhead, struck a cap filled with fulminate of mercury that exploded under the impact and sent a flash of flame down the touchhole to ignite the main powder charge. The major advantage of the system was greater reliability as neither rain or wind affected the cap.

The Percussion Principle

American military weapons were soon converted to the percussion principle. The most famous was the muzzle-loading Model 1841 rifle, otherwise known as the Yaeger (a corruption of the German *Jager*, or hunter), Harper's Ferry, or Mississippi Rifle. It was used in the Mexican War and remained in service right through the Civil War in both its original version and the improved Model 1855 with a Maynard Tape primer rather than individual percussion caps.

Over the same period, many Kentucky rifles were modified to pill lock configuration: the priming pan was replaced by an iron bowl and the cocking piece was revised into a hammer that would detonate the priming "pill" in the bowl. Further development turned the pill lock Kentucky rifle into the Plains rifle, which was better suited to the requirements of the plainsmen west of the Mississippi River. Produced by gunsmiths such as Hawkins and Dimick in St. Louis, Missouri, the Plains rifle weighed between six and ten pounds, and had calibers ranging between ·26 and ·40 inch. The barrels were generally between 26 and 38 inches long, though some weapons had longer barrels.

services of a "skillful assistant" within the Corps of Engineers. General Simon Bernard, who had served under Napoleon, was employed and became an important figure in the program of coastal fortification authorized by Congress in an effort to avoid a repeat of defeats suffered in such areas during the War of 1812.

Crawford was also responsible for expansion and academic improvement at the U.S. Military Academy at West Point. He could perhaps have moved on to a further improvement of the regular army, but in the fall of 1816, Crawford was asked to become Secretary of the Treasury so that Madison could bring Henry Clay into the cabinet as Secretary of War. However, Clay and several other men refused the appointment. George Graham, the Department of War's chief clerk, served as Acting Secretary of War for more than 12 months until John C. Calhoun became Secretary of War on December 8, 1817. By this time, the threat of renewed war with the United Kingdom had been recognized as imaginary, and Congressional interest in the army was waning. Army strength had

declined to just 8,200 men, and Congress now proposed to cut back the authorized strength, dispose of the General Staff, and close the Military Academy. Calhoun was preparing to fight these proposals when the matter was again thrown into the spotlight by an outbreak of warfare with Indian tribes on the frontier between Georgia and the Spanish possession of East Florida.

The First Seminole War (1818)

After their defeat at the Battle of Horseshoe Bend, a group from the Creek nation had settled in Spanish Florida. These Lower Creeks, also known as the "Red Sticks" because they carried red-painted war clubs, moved into the swamplands and palmetto forests of Florida along with Seminole Indians and runaway slaves. Here they were left unmolested by the Spaniards, who effectively restricted themselves to the coastal towns of St. Augustine in the east, St. Marks in the center, and Pensacola in the west.

Operating from the Bahama Islands

As it appeared in 1813, Fort Meigs was typical of the frontier defenses of its period. However, it was built as protection against the British rather than the Indians. The fort lay on the southeastern side of the Maumee river in north western Ohio, and with Fort Stephenson it blocked the eastward advance along the southern side of Lake Erie.

1. East Battery 4. Mortar
2. Major Croghan's Battery 5. Meat House
3. Gen. Cushing's Battery 6. West Battery
7. Block Houses

FORT MEIGS, 1813
Copyright 1913 by S.H.Phillips
PHOTO by C.L.LEWIS

8. Lookout 12. Britch Battery
9. Kentucky Blues Burial Ground
10. Magazines 13. Well
14. Traverse

U.S. Army, 1st Rifle Regiment, 1814

The men of the 1st Rifle Regiment wore green coats with facings of black, yellow collar lace, and yellow metal buttons. In the summer white linen leg wear was sported; but in winter, green woolen overalls were worn. The weapon was the Model 1803 rifle, and ammunition was stowed in a ''belly'' box, shot pouch and powder horn. The noncommissioned officers were similarly dressed but were distinguished by yellow worsted epaulets. In 1814, the 2nd, 3rd, and 4th Rifle Regiments were raised. There was a shortage of green woolen cloth available, so the new regiments were initially uniformed in green linen hunting smocks, soon replaced by gray uniforms.

east of Florida, two British adventurers intervened to cause trouble. Lieutenant Colonel Edward Nicholls had employed some of these Indians for an attack on Mobile in the summer of 1814 during the War of 1812. The attack had been unsuccessful. On departing for England in 1815, Nicholls left most of the weapons he had supplied for the expedition with the Indians. The other adventurer was a trader named Arbuthnot. These two persuasive Britons convinced the Indians of a complete lie. They told the tribes that the Treaty of Ghent, which ended the War of 1812, had restored to the Indians the land in southern Georgia which they had given up to the United States in the Treaty of Fort Jackson that ended the Creek War. The Indians therefore concluded that Americans were settling on land that was rightfully theirs.

A typical pattern of Indian warfare began to unfold as settlers were killed and their homesteads burned by parties

A piece of artillery equipment much used in North America was the British 6-pounder field gun, made up of a comparatively light metal ordnance on a simple two-wheeled carriage towed behind a two-wheel ammunition limber. At the top left of the illustration are three types of ammunition, namely canister (left), grapeshot (center) and round shot. Underneath the limber are the vent clearer (top) and the linstock, complete with slow match. Below the gun itself are (from top to bottom) the worm for extracting items lodged down the barrel, the rammer, the scoop, and the traversing spike.

of irate Indians. The U.S. administration tried to control the situation, principally by reinforcing Fort Scott. This post was a log structure in the southwestern corner of Georgia where the Chattahoochee and Flint rivers combine to create the Apalachicola. This river runs through Florida to the Gulf of Mexico and, at that time, was the main route of supply to the fort from Mobile and New Orleans. In November 1817, the Indians attacked a keelboat making its way up the river to

Fort Scott ahead of several supply boats, and killed or captured 34 of the 40 people on board, all soldiers or the wives of soldiers. At about the same time, a detachment of the regular army from Fort Scott attacked the Negro Fort (so called because it was garrisoned mainly by escaped slaves) on the Apalachicola River and destroyed it, thereby easing waterborne communication between Fort Scott and the coast. But with their main strength based in Spanish Florida, the

Indians were able to continue their campaign of raiding into American territory, massacring and pillaging white settlements and homesteads.

Jackson Ordered Into Action

Information about the attack on the keelboat reached Washington on December 26, 1817, and set off the First Seminole War. Secretary of War Calhoun ordered Andrew Jackson to move immediately from Nashville, Tennessee, and take personal command of Fort Scott, a garrison of 800 regular soldiers and about 1,000 Georgia militiamen. Jackson was authorized to call for more militiamen if he thought the situation warranted it. He had anticipated the nature of the trouble likely to break out in Florida and had already prepared his plans. Believing that the three-month service of the Georgia militiamen might expire by the time he reached Fort Scott, Jackson appealed for 1,000 west Tennessee volunteers for six-month service. He set off for Fort Scott with two companies of mounted militiamen, ordering the rest of his force to follow as rapidly as possible. Ahead of him, he sent an officer to Fort Hawkins in central Georgia with money to buy provisions in addition to those he had ordered from New Orleans. The supplies from New Orleans were to be moved by ship to Mobile and then farther along the coast before traveling up the Apalachicola to Fort Scott.

The sensational illustrations of eastern magazines helped to establish in urban minds the wild nature of the western frontier. This is entitled "The Sioux Massacre at Big Stone Lake, Minnesota."

The commander of the Division of the South reached Fort Hawkins on February 9, 1818, and found that the civilian contractor had failed to supply the food that had been promised. After sending an angry letter to Calhoun and managing to buy some pigs, peanuts, and corn locally, Jackson pressed on toward Fort Scott, where he arrived on March 9 and broke the Indians' siege of the fort. Here, he learned that the supply ships from Mobile had arrived at the mouth of the Apalachicola River. Jackson felt that the protection of these ships from Indian attack was vital to the success of his whole campaign, and on the following morning, he marched south down the eastern bank of the river with 400 regulars and the Georgia militiamen from Fort Scott. After six days of hard marching, the force arrived at the mouth of the Apalachicola, where there was no sign of the supply ships. Jackson decided to wait and ordered Lieutenant James Gadsen of the Corps of Engineers to build a fort for the storage of the supplies once they arrived.

The supply ships had been delayed by storms, and finally arrived on March 25. Jackson was now ready to unleash his campaign, which began on March 26 without any further delay. Jackson's plan was centered on the destruction of the Indians' main bases wherever they might be. His first objective was the Indian settlement on the Suwannee River about 150 miles to the east, where Chief Billy Bowlegs of the Seminoles was reported to be assembling a force of several thousand Indians and escaped slaves. Fort Gadsen was too far away from the Suwannee River to be a useful base, so Jackson decided to take St. Marks as a forward base. Jackson had about 1,200 men under his immediate command and, after ordering his supply ships to make for Apalachee Bay off St. Marks, moved into Spanish East Florida. The advance was delayed by the need to build canoes in

Magazine illustrations were produced to boost sales and were therefore made as lurid as possible. At the same time they may be regarded as an important part of the public information (or rather propaganda) campaigns of their periods. This "illustrates" the results of an Indian attack on the Motte family during the Seminole War.

John C. Calhoun
For further references see pages 74,82,83,100,101,103

which to cross the Ochlokonee River, and farther east by the need to root out resistance in several Indian villages, but St. Marks was taken on April 7. Here the Americans captured Arbuthnot, who was thrown into jail. Jackson's strength had already been increased by the arrival of some Tennessee volunteers as well as a sizeable party of friendly Upper Creeks, but the main body of Tennessee volunteers had inevitably been delayed by supply problems and joined the commander only on April 11. By this time, Jackson was pressing inland through the swamps to reach the main Indian settlement, the so-called Bowlegs' Town.

The Indians Escape

The Indians had been warned by Arbuthnot before his capture and had departed to safer havens. However, Jackson's men did capture a large quantity of corn and cattle with which to feed themselves. They also seized a third British adventurer from the Bahamas, Robert Armbrister, who

had been drilling Bowleg's men and teaching them about firearms. Armbrister was sent back to St. Marks, where he and Arbuthnot were tried by a military court, convicted, and executed. Jackson released his Georgia militiamen and the Upper Creeks, and headed west with his regulars and the Tennessee volunteers. Resistance in Seminole and Lower Creek villages was being broken by a number of columns. At Fort Gadsen in early May, Jackson learned that Bowlegs was assembling a force at Pensacola in the extreme west of Spanish East Florida for a final effort against the American force. Jackson took Pensacola on May 24 before the Indians could build a formidable force. The Spanish governor fled to Fort Barrancas, but Jackson's artillery shelled the position and forced the surrender of the governor and his Spanish troops. In Pensacola, Jackson established an American garrison to match that in St. Marks, and toward the end of the month he departed for Nashville.

The First Seminole War had succeeded in its main objective, which was the

Another example of the same journalistic style is "American Frontier Life." Here, frontiersmen spring an ambush on Indians drawn into the light of a campfire by three dummies.

The Seminoles

For further references see pages 79, 82, 105, *107*, 108, *109, 110, 112*, 114, *115*, 117, 118

U.S. Army, 6th Regiment, Private, 1814

In June 1812, the War of 1812 began, and a month later, the strength of the army stood at only 6,686 men out of an authorized establishment of 35,603. The regular establishment of the U.S. Army was soon expanded greatly, though the 37 new regiments nominally raised in 1812 and 1813 were at first no better than the state militia units beside which they served. Even though the new regiments were greatly below strength, it was impossible to supply the men with proper uniforms, and shortages of blue woolen cloth forced the Purveyor of Public Supplies to issue substitute uniforms of several different types. Gray, brown, and even olive drab cloth was used, and the facings were either omitted or simplified. This private of the 6th Regiment wears the regulation "coatee" above brown linen fatigue trousers. The leather cap is of the type adopted in 1813, with a flap that could be lowered to protect the neck; the cap decorations include a metal plate, a leather cockade with a brass eagle, a tasseled cord, and a felt pom-pom on the left, though the 6th Infantry (like the Volunteers and the Marine Corps) was permitted to wear a buck's tail in place of the pom-pom.

complete destruction of Lower Creek and Seminole military capability against American settlers in Georgia. But the whole campaign had also been extremely provocative. Jackson had led American forces into Spanish territory, attacked and captured Spanish forts, and executed two British citizens. Spain and the United Kingdom could have caused considerable international trouble for the United States, but preferred not to do so. Negotiations with Spain for the purchase

River in the Gulf of Mexico northwest to the Pacific Ocean.

Logistics Again Inadequate

As far as military operations in the First Seminole War were concerned, the U.S. could only be grateful that the opposition had been so poor. Throughout the campaign, Jackson had been forced to devote most of his energy to feeding and

Not all American contacts with the Indians were bloody. This illustration shows Major Stephen H. Long listening to Indian grievances at a council of the Pawnee Indians in 1819-1820

of Florida were already under way and were finally completed by the signature of the Adams-Onis Treaty on February 19, 1819. In this treaty, the Spanish abandoned all claim to West Florida, which was already occupied by the United States, and ceded East Florida. The captured forts had been handed back to the Spanish late in 1818, but were now returned to American ownership. Other provisions of the Adams-Onis Treaty were a cancellation of all Spanish claims to the Pacific Northwest region, and the setting of the frontier between U.S. and Spanish territory from the mouth of the Sabine

otherwise maintaining his force in the field. The supply system had failed completely. The fault was traced yet again to the continued use of civilian contractors, who invariably delivered quantities of rations below those contracted, and frequently delivered the supplies after the contracted date or to the wrong place. Calhoun appealed to Congress, and in April 1818, it was decided that in the future contractors would have to deliver rations in bulk at specified depots under a better system of transportation. The Congressional measure also guaranteed stricter army control of civilian contrac-

Molds were the best way of making sure that each unit had the right caliber of bullet for its weapons. These molds could be of the single type (right) or any of several "gang" molds. With the mold closed, molten lead was poured into the open top. Once the lead had hardened, the mold was opened, and the ball(s) were extracted and cleaned, ready to use.

tors' supplies through a Subsistence Department of the type not seen since the Revolutionary War.

Secretary of War Calhoun was convinced that frontier security and operations would be better left to regular forces. He expressed this idea to a senior officer by writing that calling the militia into service was "harassing to them and exhausting to the treasury. Protection is the first object, and the second is protection by the regular force." But continued

political fears about a large regular army combined with economic factors made Calhoun's notion impractical. Any regular army was now needed to protect northern, western, and southwestern land frontiers, as well as the coastal forts of the eastern and southern seaboards.

In 1820, Calhoun was instructed by Congress to comment on a plan to reduce the regular army to a strength of only 6,000 men. Calhoun replied that any reduction would be unwise, but that if

In September 1825, Governor Lewis Cass of Michigan and William Clark of Missouri were U.S. commissioners at the signing of a great treaty at Prairie du Chien on the upper reaches of the Mississippi River in Wisconsin. This painting was done on the spot by J.O. Lewis, and purports to show the occasion *"at which upwards of 50,000 Indian Warriors of the Chippeways, Sioux, Sacs & Foxes, Winnebagoes, Pottowattomies, Menomonies, Iowats and Ottowas tribes were present."*

reduction were essential, the best course would be to reduce the strength of each company by half, leaving in existence an organization that could be flushed out rapidly during an emergency to create a 19,000-man army. It was again a far-sighted concept - in effect, the origin of the later concept of the "expansible army" - but it was rejected by Congress. Instead, it was decided on March 2, 1821, that the strength of the army's standard companies would be reduced (in the case of the infantry company from 68 to 42); and that the current establishment of eight infantry regiments, one rifle regiment, one light artillery regiment, and the eight-battalion corps of artillery would be

Typical of a ship's armament is this light 6-pounder gun on a wheeled carriage, which here is seen without all the tackle for controlling the recoil and then running out the loaded weapon. Ordnance elevation was controlled by moving the quoin (wooden wedge) under the breech. Under the gun are (from top to bottom) a scoop, worm, rammer, swab, and traverse spike. Farther to the right are (top row, left to right) the priming powder horn, linstock in a water bucket, and round shot, and (bottom row, left to right) vent prick and knife, serge powder bag, and wad.

trimmed to seven infantry regiments and four artillery regiments. At the same time, the geographical organization of the army was altered from the existing Divisions of the North and of the South to an Eastern Department commanded by Brigadier General Winfield Scott and a Western Department commanded by Brigadier General Edmund P. Gaines.

A weapon that was often mounted in boats and then in smaller warships was the carronade, a lightweight type based on a slide rather than a wheeled carriage. Designed to use only a small charge to fire a heavy ball over only a short range, the carronade was light, easy to make and therefore comparatively cheap.

Commanding General of the Army

The new establishment also allowed for only one major general. As Jackson had resigned from the army to become governor of Florida, this presented no challenge to the only other officer holding the rank, Major General Jacob Brown. To fill a
Continued on page 100

THE BEGINNINGS OF THE U.S. NAVY

From the start of the Revolutionary War, there were "warships" in American service, although they were little more than armed merchantmen operating under the auspices of the colonial armed forces. The first naval action of the Revolutionary War is now considered to have been the capture, on June 12, 1775, of the British ship *Margaretta* by the *Unity*. After hearing of the events at Concord and Lexington, Jeremiah O'Brien and about 40 men seized guns, swords, axes, and pitchforks, boarded the *Unity* in Machias Bay, Maine, and then came up with the *Margaretta* at sea. After a fierce fight, the Americans captured the British ship.

On September 5, 1775, the schooner *Hannah* became the first regularly commissioned American warship. On the very day that she was commissioned, the *Hannah* sailed; two days later, she cap-

Born in Scituate, Rhode Island, during 1718, Commodore Esek Hopkins was the first commander-in-chief of the Continental Navy, and received his appointment on December 22, 1775. His brother was chairman of the Naval Committee of the Congress. Though instructed to operate against British ships in Chesapeake Bay, Hopkins used the excuse of a rendezvous (by six of his eight ships) off the Bahamas after his squadron had become separated to make a landing on New Providence. After his return Hopkins was censured by the Continental Congress, and in the following year, he was suspended from his command. A few months later Hopkins was formally dismissed.

tured a British ship. The *Hannah* was the first vessel of "Washington's Fleet," which soon numbered five other schooners and a brigantine.

The formal birthday of the U.S. Navy is officially October 13, 1775. On this date, the Continental Congress ordered two ships to be fitted out for use in the essential task of intercepting British supplies before they reached North America. The Congress had been much impressed with the success of "Washington's Fleet," and the first step toward the creation of a Continental Navy was entrusted to Silas Deane, Christopher Gadsen, and John Langdon. The first disciplinary framework for the new service was provided by the "Rules for the Regulation of the Navy of the United Colonies," prepared by John Adams and issued on November 28, 1775. (The name "The United States" was not adopted until September 6, 1776.)

The First Union Flag to Fly From an American Warship

On December 3, 1775, Lieutenant John Paul Jones hoisted the Grand Union flag (13 American stripes with the Union flag in the field) on his ship, the *Alfred,* the first occasion on which a flag had been unfurled on an American warship. Ten days later, the Continental Congress ordered the building of 13 warships for the Continental Navy. Only seven of them were completed, and all were lost in the Revolutionary War. The ships ordered were all frigates: five of 32 guns each, five of 28 guns each, and three of 24 guns each. The order also stipulated where the ships were to be built, to spread the work among the 13 colonies. Further progress in the establishment of the Continental Navy was made on December 22 of the same year, when Esek Hopkins was appointed commander-in-chief, making him the Continental Navy's equivalent of Major General George Washington in the Continental Army. (Only two years later, however, Hopkins was court-martialed for failure to obey orders and dismissed from

the service.) In the short term, the Continental Navy had at its disposal four ships, which were soon joined by four converted merchantmen.

On January 5, 1776, this first fleet of the Continental Navy received its sailing orders: Hopkins was instructed to drive British raiders from Chesapeake Bay as well as the coasts of the Carolinas and Virginia. The American commander sailed from the Delaware River on February 17 with eight ships. After losing contact with two ships in foul weather, Hopkins made for the Bahama Islands, where the navy and marine raid on New Providence was undertaken. Returning from the Bahamas, Captain Abraham Whipple's 24-gun armed merchantman *Columbus* captured a British schooner, the *Hawk,* off Block Island, Rhode Island, the first action with a British warship in the Revolutionary War. The *Columbus* captured a total of five British ships before being run aground and burned in 1778.

A typical recruiting poster of the period urges men to come forward as crew of John Paul Jones's sloop *Ranger,* which was about to depart on a raiding voyage in English waters.

GREAT ENCOURAGEMENT FOR SEAMEN.

ALL GENTLEMEN SEAMEN and able-bodied LANDSMEN who have a Mind to diſtinguiſh themſelves in the GLORIOUS CAUSE of their COUNTRY, and make their Fortunes, an Opportunity now offers on board the Ship RANGER, of Twenty Guns, (for FRANCE) now laying in PORTSMOUTH, in the State of NEW-HAMPSHIRE, commanded by JOHN PAUL JONES Eſq; let them repair to the Ship's Rendezvous in PORTSMOUTH, or at the Sign of Commodore MANLEY, in SALEM, where they will be kindly entertained, and receive the greateſt Encouragement.---The Ship RANGER, in the Opinion of every Perſon who has ſeen her is looked upon to be one of the beſt Cruizers in AMERICA.---She will be always able to Fight her Guns under a moſt excellent Cover ; and no Veſſel yet built was ever calculated for ſailing faſter, and making good Weather.

Any GENTLEMEN VOLUNTEERS who have a Mind to take an agreable Voyage in this pleaſant Seaſon of the Year, may, by entering on board the above Ship RANGER, meet with every Civility they can poſſibly expect, and for a further Encouragement depend on the firſt Opportunity being embraced to reward each one agreable to his Merit.

All reaſonable Travelling Expences will be allowed, and the Advance-Money be paid on their Appearance on Board.

IN CONGRESS, MARCH 29, 1777.

RESOLVED,

THAT the MARINE COMMITTEE be authoriſed to advance to every able Seaman, that enters into the CONTINENTAL SERVICE, any Sum not exceeding FORTY DOLLARS, and to every ordinary Seaman or Landſman, any Sum not exceeding TWENTY DOLLARS, to be deducted from their future Prize-Money.

By Order of CONGRESS,

JOHN-HANCOCK, PRESIDENT.

On September 5, 1776, the first standard uniform was adopted by the Marine Committee of the Continental Congress: naval officers were to have green coats with white facings, round cuffs with buttons, slashed sleeves and pockets, a silver epaulet on the right shoulder, turned-back shirt collars, buttons matching the facings, vest and breeches edged in green, black gaiters, and garters.

On November 13, 1776, John Paul Jones, captaining the brig *Providence*, took the transport *Mellish*, which was carrying 10,000 winter uniforms for British forces fighting in the Revolutionary War. This clothing was a godsend to the Continental land forces. Later, as he was escorting eight prizes to port, Jones fell in with the frigate H.M.S. *Milford*, which he persuaded to chase his American warship, thereby leaving the prizes free to enter an American port. Jones later evaded the British frigate and returned safely to harbor. It was also Jones who unfurled the first "Stars and Stripes" on a Continental warship, at Portsmouth, New Hampshire, on July 4, 1777.

The Capture of the *Lexington*

The first American warship to be captured overseas was the *Lexington* (originally the *Wild Duck*) on September 20, 1777. Encountering the cutter *Alert* off Ushant, France, the *Lexington* fought bravely until she had fired off all her powder and then, with her rigging shot to pieces, surrendered. A greater blow happened on March 7, 1778, when the frigate *Randolph* took on the British 64-gun ship H.M.S. *Yarmouth*. The American ship was apparently on the point of victory, but blew up for unknown reasons (perhaps a spark in the powder magazine) with the loss of 300 men. It was the worst disaster to befall an American warship until Pearl Harbor in December 1941.

On May 4, 1880, the Continental Congress authorized the first navy seal. It was in effect designed by Governor Morris and Richard Henry Lee, members of the committee charged with producing for the use of the Board of Admiralty, forerunner of the Department ment of the Navy, which was itself established in 1798.

The Last Naval Action of the Revolutionary War

The final naval action of the Revolutionary War was the inconclusive battle fought on March 10, 1783, between the 36-gun frigate *Alliance* and H.M.S. *Sybil*, the latter with H.M.S. *Alarm* and H.M.S. *Tobago* in company. News of the war's end had not reached the ships, and the *Alliance* badly damaged the *Sybil* with a single broadside. The British ship then hauled off to join her companions, which did not take part in the action. The losses of the Continental Navy in the Revolutionary War totaled 342 dead and 114 wounded.

Top: The first ship commanded by Captain John Barry in the Continental Navy was the brigantine *Wild Duck*, bought into the navy and renamed *Lexington*. Like John Paul Jones, Barry had been born in Ireland and was second only to Jones in the fame of his actions in the Revolutionary War. **Above:** The "Stars and Stripes" is hoisted for the first time on an American warship, John Paul Jones's *Lexington*, on July 4, 1777.

The Continental Navy effectively ceased to exist on June 2, 1785, when the service's last ship, the *Alliance*, was sold for merchant service. It was nine years before another U.S. navy started to come into existence. However, on August 4, 1790, Congress authorized the creation of the Revenue Cutter Service. This later became the U.S. Coast Gaurd, so the date of the Revenue Cutter Service's creation is generally recognized as the birthday of the Coast Guard.

By the middle of the 1790s, the activities of Barbary Coast pirates off North Africa were becoming a major thorn in the side of American merchant ships trading in the Mediterranean. On January 2, 1794, Congress resolved to create a United States navy to deal with these Algerine corsairs. Opponents of the plan were both numerous and influential. They pointed out that such a service would be very expensive, aristocratic in its overall nature, detrimental to democratic ideals, and officered by glory-hunters whose efforts could drag the country into unwanted overseas wars.

The Birth of the U.S. Navy

March 27, 1794, is generally regarded as the birthday of the U.S. Navy, for on that day the Congress ordered the building of nine frigates, six of them of 44 guns each and the other three of 36 guns each. The order was accompanied by the condition that the building program would be cancelled if peace with the Algerine corsairs was secured.

The order for these new ships was awarded on June 28, 1794, to Joshua Humphreys, a major shipbuilder of Philadelphia. Humphreys was appointed master builder at a salary of $2,000 per year, and the ships included such legendary vessels as the *Constellation*, *Constitution*, and *United States*. However, on March 2, 1796, Congress ratified a treaty with the Bey of Algiers. In addition to halting the construction of the ships, the treaty gave $1 million to the bey in ransom and tribute.

The navy survived this blow, however, and on February 22, 1796, President George Washington conferred the first U.S. U.S. Navy commission on Captain John Barry, a merchant who had commanded the brig *Lexington* in March 1776 when she captured the British tender *Edward* in the Continental Navy's first successful sea action. Barry's first command was the *United States*, which had been designed by Humphreys and Captain Thomas Truxtun, launched on May 10, 1797, and remained in service until 1864.

The Quasi-War With France

The fortunes of the navy began to climb once more with the "outbreak" of the Quasi-War with France. The first evidence of this improvement was the establishment on April 30, 1798, of the Department of the Navy under a Secretary of the Navy. Only a few days later, Congress authorized President John Adams to build or buy ten ships, "galleys or otherwise," for the defense of the United States, and also permitted the captains of armed public vessels to raid French merchant shipping. The first Secretary of the Navy was Benjamin Stoddert, who was appointed on May 18, 1798. In the next two years, Stoddert increased the Navy's strength to more than 50 vessels, including many allocated to the West Indies, where piracy was a major problem.

The Quasi-War with France was fought on an undeclared basis, and one of its high points was the capture, on July 7, 1798, of the French privateer *La Croyable* off Great Egg Harbor in the Delaware Capes region by the *Delaware* under the command of Captain Stephen Decatur, Sr. This event led to the first award of prize money by the U.S. Navy. The first warship-versus-warship success claimed by the U.S. Navy followed on February 9, 1799, when the *Constellation* captured the French frigate *L'Insurgente* in the Caribbean: raked by a devastating broadside that killed 29 men, the French frigate surrendered.

The navy also entered the shipbuilding market when it bought the 60-acre

U.S.S. *Constitution*
Type: 44-gun sailing frigate
Displacement: 2,200 tons
 full load
Dimensions: length 204 ft.
 overall and 175 ft. on the
 gun deck;
 beam 45 ft.;
 draft 20 ft.;
 depth of hold 14 ft. 3 in.
Masts: foremast 94 ft.;
 mainmast 104 ft.;
 mizzenmast 81 ft.
Speed: 13 knots
Crew: about 500

The first ships of the U.S. Navy, authorized by Congress in March 1794, are often known as the "six original frigates." They were the *United States*, *Constitution*, *President*, *Chesapeake*, *Constellation* and *Congress*. Their dimensions were fixed by three of the captains (John Barry, Richard Dale and Thomas Truxtun) commissioned by President George Washington to command them. The most famous of these celebrated ships is the *Constitution*, which was built at Hartt's Shipyard in Boston, Massachusetts; launched on October 21, 1797; and commissioned on an unknown date in 1798. The ship first put to sea on July 22, 1798, during the Quasi-War with France, and then served as Commodore Edward Preble's flagship in the Mediterranean during the Tripolitanian War. However, it was during the War of 1812 that the *Constitution* achieved her undying fame as Captain Isaac Hull's "Old Ironsides" during her action with the *Guerriere*. Under Captain William Bainbridge, the *Constitution* captured the *Java*, another British frigate, off Brazil on December 29, 1812. On February 20, 1815, under the command of Captain Charles Stewart, the ship fought a four-hour battle and captured two smaller British ships, the 32-gun *Cyane* and the 20-gun *Levant*. In 1828, the *Constitution* was condemned as unseaworthy and recommended for breaking up. The poem "Old Ironsides" by Oliver Wendell Holmes raised such public enthusiasm for the ship, however, that she was preserved. The ship has been rebuilt several times and restored as much as possible to her original configuration. Between 1917 and 1925, the ship was known as the *Old Constitution*, allowing allocation of her original name to a battle-cruiser that was never completed.

The *Constitution*'s last major reconstruction took place between 1927 and 1931, after which the ship toured some 90 American ports and received 4,500,000 visitors. Since 1934, the *Constitution* has been moored at the Boston Naval Shipyard and is the oldest commissioned warship still afloat. Twice each year, the ship is taken out into Boston Harbor and "turned around" so that her masts do not warp from the effects of the wind and sun.

yard of Mr. and Mrs. William Dennet in Prtsmouth, New Hampshire, for $5,500 on June 12, 1800. The yard had already built warships; it later became the Portsmouth Navy Yard.

The best known single event contributing to the outbreak of the War of 1812 occured on June 22, 1807, when the frigate HMS *Leopard* fired at the *Chesapeake* off Norfolk, Virginia, killing three and wounding 18 of the American frigate's crew before impressing other of her men. War was declared by Congress on June 18, 1812. Sixteen ships were faced by a Royal Navy that had 1,048 vessels in commission, though very large numbers of these British ships were committed in other parts of the world, especially in the Napoleonic War with France. Navy losses in the War of 1812 amounted to 265 killed and 439 wounded.

New Technology

The period was also notable for the development of new technology, exemplified by the launch, on October 29, 1814 of the first steam warship, generally known as the *Fulton*, but more formally designated *Demologos (Fulton I)*. This pioneering ship driven by a centerwheel paddle, was planned with an armament of 30 32-pounder cannon and two 100-pounder Columbia guns for her harbor-defense role. The War of 1812 ended before the ship was completed, and she was finally fitted out as a receiving vessel. Designed by Robert Fulton, the ship came to an unfortunate end, at Brooklyn Navy Yard on June 4, 1829, when her magazine blew up, totally destroying the vessel and killing 30 men, as well as injuring many more.

The battle between the American ship *Planter* and a French privateer during the Quasi-War with France. This undeclared war was very popular in the navy because all ranks received prize money from the sale of captured ships. During the conflicts, the fighting strength of the navy reached 45 ships.

Above right: In the early days of the U.S. Navy, American ships generally won single-ship duels because of their superior gunnery.

Below: A classic engagement of the War of 1812 was the victory of the 44-gun *Constitution*, under Captain Isaac Hull, over the 48-gun *Guerriere* on August 19, 1812. The *Constitution* was the third of the "six original frigates" ordered in 1794 and was built with spikes and copper bolts supplied by Paul Revere. The ship was nicknamed "Old Ironsides" by her sailors because the shot from the *Guerriere* failed to pierce her sides.

The United States was a pioneer of steam propulsion for ships. The world's first commercial steam vessel was Robert Fulton's *Clermont*, which steamed up the Hudson River from New York to Albany during 1807 (above), and in 1814 the navy bought its first steam warship.

On March 3, 1819, Congress passed legislation that materially affected the navy. First, rules about the naming of warships specified that ships of the line were to be named after states, frigates after rivers, and sloops after cities. Second, a stepped-up war against pirates who were capturing hundreds of American ships every year was authorized. The worst area for piracy was the Caribbean, and the new law gave permission for the navy to escort merchant convoys and to recapture ships seized by pirates. Third, the president was authorized to use the navy to suppress the West African slave trade.

The navy's second steamship, and the first to serve as a warship, was the *Sea Gull*. The shallow-draft ship had been bought in December 1822, and on February 14, 1823, was commissioned under Lieutenant William H. Watson as a shallow-draft warship capable of operating against pirates along the Cuban coast.

The Navy Expands

In 1825, Congress authorized the construction of a class of ten sloops. On September 3, 1826, one of them, the 700-ton *Vincennes* of 16 guns, left New York under the command of Commander William B. Finch. It became the first American naval vessel to circumnavigate the world before returning to New York on June 8, 1830. Just under six months later, on December 6, 1830, the navy established a Depot of Charts and Instruments under Lieutenant Fontain Maury. This important scientific adjunct of the navy became the US Naval and Hydrographic Office in 1854 and the U.S. Naval Oceanographic Office in 1862.

The first official controls for the dress of enlisted naval personnel were issued on February 1, 1841, and this "Regulation for the Uniform and Dress of the Navy of the United States" ended the practice of men being able to decorate their "frocks"

Captain, U.S. Navy, 1862

This captain of the Union navy is seen in typical undress uniform for the 1862 period, complete with straw hat of the type worn in southern waters. At this time, the world's navies were beginning to accept the implications of steam power for warships, and in the relatively unpompous U.S. navies there was no hinderance to the appearance of officers in uniforms of a practical, rather than ceremonial nature.

A hero of the U.S. Navy's early period was Captain Stephen Decatur, who secured great fame for his success against the Barbary corsairs and also against the British. He was killed in a duel during 1820.

Sailors from the *Constitution* board and take the French privateer *Sandwich* in the West Indies during May 1800.

The *United States* was launched on May 10, 1797, as the first of the U.S. Navy's "six "six original frigates." She is seen here as she appeared when she was commissioned later in the same year under the command of Captain John Barry, who had overseen the ship's construction. Her hulk was seized by the Confederacy at Norfolk Navy Yard in 1861 and used as a receiving ship (moored training vessel), but was burned when the Confederates evacuated Norfolk in 1862.

as they wished. It also established the device of a spread eagle on the stock of a foul anchor as the insignia of petty officers.

Mutiny

The navy's only mutiny occurred on December 1, 1842, on board the training brig *Somers*. The three persons involved, Midshipman Philip Spencer (son of the Secretary of War) and two enlisted men, were court-martialed for conspiracy to mutiny, found guilty, and hanged on the orders of their captain, Alexander S. McKenzie, who was later court-martialed and acquitted.

The End of Flogging

The Naval School, now the United States Naval Academy, was founded at Anapolis, Maryland, on October 10, 1845, with Commander Franklin Buchanan as its superintendent. The school's initial complement was seven staff and 56 students. Five years later, on September 28, 1850, Congress moved toward the abolition of flogging as a naval punishment. The navy said that it would be "utterly impractical to have an efficient Navy without this form of practice," but on July 17, 1862, flogging was finally banned, even though sailors had petitioned Congress not to erfd the practice. Between this date and the beginning of the Civil War, the most notable event in naval history, apart from small-scale operations mainly in the Pacific, was the decision announced on November 1, 1860, to convert seven sail-powered warships into steam-driven ships at a cost of $3,064,000.

Continued from page 87

gap in the chain of command that had become evident in the War of 1812, Brown was brought to Washington in a position between the Department of War and the army that later became known as Commanding General of the Army. This appointment was held by Brown until his death in 1828. Major General Alexander Macomb then held the position until his death in 1841, when he was replaced by Major General Winfield Scott. In 1847, Scott was promoted to brevet lieutenant general, and as the first lieutenant general since Washington, he remained Commanding General of the Army until he retired in 1861.

Calhoun's Great Importance

It is difficult to overestimate the importance of Secretary of War Calhoun in American military affairs. The vision and energy of this important official were very great and allowed responsible officers to use their administrative skills to maximum extent. Scott began working on the difficult problem of infantry tactics in 1815, and he eventually issued a new manual of infantry tactics for the army and militia. In 1821, the same officer prepared a new set of army regulations that detailed to the smallest item how the lives of the men were to be ordered. In 1822, the army began opening recruiting posts in larger cities to recruit for the army in general instead of recruiting for specific regiments as it had previously done. Regimental recruitment was allowed to continue, but in its first three years, the General Recruiting Service enlisted nearly 70 percent more men than the regimental recruiting offices. At Calhoun's instigation, an improved medical service was established under Joseph Lovell, the first commissioned Surgeon General.

A contemporary illustration of Fort Mellon on Lake Monroe in East Florida emphasizes the unusual aspect of this location. What it cannot even begin to suggest, however, are the nature and extent of the region's endemic diseases. They caused far more American casualties in the Florida campaigns than Indian weapons.

Swivel guns were used where more fire power than a musket, but less than a heavy cannon was required. Often mounted in boats or along bulwarks, they could fire devastating ball or grapeshot into other boats or at infantry on beaches. Some were fitted into the fighting tops of ships to fire down onto the decks of others about to attempt boarding. The swivel gun shown bottom right was designed to fire a large explosive (fuzed) ball against a target.

Lovell was instrumental in improving the soldier's diet, and in his search for a link between climate and disease, he created the basis of the world's first national weather reporting service.

As early as 1818, Calhoun had been able to put into effect the army's first complete artillery system involving all three branches of the service, namely field artillery, siege and garrison artillery, and coastal artillery. This amalgamation resulted from the deliberations of a board of artillery and ordnance officers appointed by Calhoun. Field artillery was based in general on a twin-trail carriage devised by a late 18th-century French artillery pioneer, Jean Baptiste de Gribeauval, though in 1839, Secretary of War Joel R. Poinsett approved a revised type of stock-trail carriage with a single trail of solid wood. It had been introduced by the British but perfected by the French, and offered both superior interchangeability of parts and greater simplicity than the 1818 type of carriage.

These organizational, administrative, and technical improvements were matched by a major program to better the nation's coastal defenses. By 1826, 26 ports between the Penobscot River in Maine and the mouth of the Mississippi River in Louisiana had been fortified with

31 works, generally grass-covered earthworks backed by stone or masonry walls. By 1843, the program had been stretched to cover 35 to 40 ports, with 69 large fortifications built or under construction containing heavy artillery in the form of 24- and 32-pounder guns as well as 8-inch howitzers to match the heavier firepower of contemporary warships.

Westward Expansion

Throughout this period, the westward expansion of the United States seemed relentless as settlers searched for new land. The army moved in front of the settlers, and the 30 years after 1815 saw the army in constant service as the pioneer of westward expansion. Soldiers surveyed, built forts, and constructed roads. Army posts in Iowa, Nebraska, and Kansas marked the western edge of American endeavor, and outside its forts, the army set up the blacksmith forges and lumber and corn-grinding mills that were a powerful focus for civilian settlement. Typical of these army posts, by geographical location from north to south, were Forts Armstrong, Snelling, and Atkinson built on the upper reaches

U.S. Military Academy, Cadet, 1825

The U.S. Military Academy was founded in 1802 at West Point, New York. By 1825, it was well established and developing into a far-sighted educational and training establishment for some 250 cadets under the overall command of Sylvanus Thayer. The uniform of the cadets, adopted in 1815 or 1816, was of gray cloth in honor of the gray-clad regulars who had beaten the British at the Battle of Chippewa in July 1814. White cross belts were worn for infantry drill, while a black waist belt and straight sword were normal for other occasions. The cadets used a shorter musket than the standard for line infantry, and other uniform and equipment items were modified to suit the cadets.

of the Mississippi River in 1819, 1822, and 1840 respectively, Fort Leavenworth built on the Missouri River in 1827, Fort Scott built between the Missouri and Arkansas rivers in 1842, Forts Smith and Gibson built on the Arkansas River in 1817 and 1824 respectively, Forts Towson and Washita built on the Red River in 1824 and 1842 respectively, and Fort Jesup built on the Sabine River in 1822. The main base for the supply and reinforcement of the more northern forts was the Jefferson Barracks, erected in St. Louis in 1826.

In addition to opening up new frontier regions for settlement, these army forts were also the launching points for expeditions deeper into the west. From Fort Leavenworth, for example, army expeditions surveyed the Santa Fe and Oregon Trails that opened the way to the southwest and northwest respectively. Another celebrated expedition was that of Captain Benjamin L. E. Bonneville, who during the 1830s took four years leave of absence from the 7th Infantry Regiment for an exploration of the Pacific coast.

This first phase of expansion into the midwest was undertaken mainly by infantrymen. Where possible, they were transported in steamboats, and then when the terrain permitted by mule- or ox-drawn wagons, but ultimately they covered the worst terrain on foot. Then the army discovered that the Plains Indians were mounted, and in 1832, the army organized a battalion of mounted rangers, expanded during 1833 into the 1st Dragoon Regiment, the first cavalry in the regular army since 1815.

In 1831, the army received as its political head Lewis Cass, previously governor of Michigan and eventually the first Secretary of War since Calhoun to serve over a long period. Like Calhoun, Cass had barely settled into office before he was faced with an Indian war.

The Black Hawk War (1832)

In 1824, the Erie Canal had been opened,

Painted from life in 1833 by J.O. Lewis, this impressive man was the chief of the Sac Indians. Known to the Americans as Black Hawk, his formal title was Mac-Cut-I-Mish-E-Ca-Cu-Cac.

Major General Zachary Taylor, seen here in a painting attributed to Lambdin, had a long military career that culminated in the Mexican War of 1846-1848. His success produced a wave of public enthusiasm that catapulted him into the White House as the twelfth president. In the Black Hawk War, Taylor was a colonel and victor in the decisive Battle of Bad Axe River.

encouraging a flood of immigration into Illinois. By 1831 this flood had reached the lands of the Fox and Sac tribes in western Illinois, pushing the Indians west across the Mississippi River into the prairies. Not unnaturally, the Indians were very unhappy with this situation, and under Chief Black Hawk, a group of Sac Indians crossed the Mississippi River in the spring of 1831 in a raid that burned the homesteads of many settlers. This Sac band was sometimes called the "British Band" because it had served with the British in the War of 1812. Its activities in 1831 prompted a major response from the Department of the West. Gaines moved against the Sacs with a large force of regulars and volunteers, but Black Hawk merely retired back across the

Mississippi River and left Gaines' force with no military objective.

In the following year, Black Hawk decided that the time had come for a bolder move. In April 1832, he again crossed the Mississippi River, intending to re-occupy the ancestral Sac lands. In addition to 500 warriors, he brought with him 1,500 women and children. Cass decided that only a major show of force would settle the incipient Indian problem of the area. Accordingly, he instructed Colonel Henry Atkinson to move up the Mississippi River from Jefferson Barracks in St. Louis with the 6th Infantry Regiment and ordered General Scott to move about 1,000 more infantry and some artillery from the east coast. He reckoned that this combined force would be more than

BLACK HAWK

PROPHET.   SON.

Chief Black Hawk and his two sons. It is estimated that between 850 and 1,400 Sacs died in the Battle of Bad Axe River or drowned after being hounded into the local marshes after the battle. Black Hawk tried to surrender, but his plea was ignored by the Americans, who were still smarting from a trick played on them by Black Hawk in an earlier engagement, the Battle of Wisconsin Heights. The battle has since become known as the Bad Axe Massacre, and in 1990 the state legislature of Wisconsin issued a proclamation of apology to the Sac and Fox nations.

adequate to defeat Black Hawk, and also to instill in the tribes of the area a fear of American military strength. To supplement these regular forces, the governor of Illinois Mississippi called out a major part of his militia, most of them mounted.

The Battle of Bad Axe River

The Illinois militia had an early and inconclusive encounter with the Sacs, and most of the militia then returned home. Atkinson had meanwhile been moving north with about 500 regulars and about 900 volunteers, as many as he had been able to muster. Advancing with great difficulty through swampland, Atkinson's force caught up with the Indians on August 2 in the area of southern Wisconsin where the Bad Axe River flows into the Mississippi. The main infantry force was commanded by Colonel Zachary Taylor and decisively beat the Indians, who were

also decimated by canister shot from a 6-pounder field gun mounted on a steamboat.

Scott's force from the east coast only arrived five days later, but would in any event have been next to useless. Cholera had broken out on the transports ferrying the force across the Great Lakes: one-third of Scott's men had died of the disease or been left as invalids, while many of the others had desrted. The rest could not be brought into contact with Atkinson's men for fear of contagion.

The Second Seminole War (1835-42)

Even as the Black Hawk War was taking place, fresh trouble was brewing among the Creeks and Seminoles of Georgia, Florida, and Alabama. Early in 1832, Cass instructed the Indian commissioner in Florida to negotiate a treaty with the Indians, which was ratified in 1834. In the

Left: Determined to remain in their ancestral lands after returning across the Mississippi River, Black Hawk brought 500 warriors, together with 1,500 women and children who were a great tactical burden on the Indian chief at the time of the Battle of Bad Axe River.

Below: The decisive factor in the Battle of Bad Axe River was the steam vessel *Warrior* with a 6-pounder field gun mounted on her bow and firing canister. This consists of a mass of musket balls that spread out into a lethal cloud as their container breaks up as it leaves the gun muzzle.

Painted by the great George Catlin, Osceola was a half breed who led the Seminoles in their protracted effort in the Second Seminole War to avoid forcible removal to the west from southern Georgia and northern Florida. After their defeat, the surviving Seminoles were shipped to New Orleans and then moved into Arkansas and Oklahoma.

Texas
For further references
see pages
43,46,116,120,121,
122,123,124,125,126,
127,128

treaty, the Indians agreed to move from Florida to Arkansas by January 1, 1836, but long before this date, it became clear that many Seminoles were not prepared to move peaceably. There were several outbreaks of minor violence organized by a half–breed named Osceola, and the army decided that reinforcement of its Florida forces was needed. By December 1835, the army had 536 men in Florida, organized as two companies of infantry and nine companies of artillery under Brevet Brigadier General Duncan L. Clinch. The two main garrisons were Fort Brooke on Tampa Bay and Fort King about 100 miles to the northeast.

The decisive moment arrived on December 28, 1835. A party of 60 men under Osceola murdered the agent in charge of the Indian move as he took a walk outside Fort King. Another group of Indians attacked a party of 110 regulars under the command of Brevet Major Francis L. Dade as they were marching toward Fort King from Fort Brooke. The force was moving slowly through the Wahoo Swamp of the Withlacoochee River because they had with them an ox-drawn 6-pounder field gun; only two soldiers escaped alive (but badly wounded) from the "Dade Massacre."

Such outrages could not go unavenged and unpunished, and so the Second Seminole War began. The massacre had taken place just west of the line separating the Departments of the East and the West, and therefore fell theoretically into General Gaines' area of responsibility. But Secretary of War Cass and President Andrew Jackson agreed that command should be given to General Scott. Gaines, currently on a tour of inspection in New Orleans, was ordered to the southwestern frontier to assume command of troops in Louisiana, into Texas where trouble was brewing between American immigrants and Mexico, which had declared itself independent of Spain in February 1821.

Scott departed from Washington on January 21, 1836. In South Carolina and Georgia, he ordered supplies and arranged for the state militias to be called into service. He also established a supply base in Savannah, Georgia, and arrived at his new headquarters in St. Augustine, on the opposite side of the Florida peninsula from the scene of operations, on February 22. Supply and other logistical difficulties, including the movement of troops across the difficult and largely unexplored interior of Florida, delayed the start of the American campaign until April 5. Scott's plan was to undertake a three-pronged offensive designed to trap the Indians close to Tampa, but by the time he was ready, the Indians had disappeared into the swamps of the Everglades. To add to Scott's problems, hot weather had arrived, and his militia forces were ready to return home as they had completed their three-month period of active service. This first stage of the war was accurately summarized by a South

Carolina militia officer: ''Two months were consumed in preparations and effecting nothing, and the third in marching to Tampa and back again.''

Differences Between the First and Second Seminole Wars

It is worth noting at this stage that, while Scott's initial experience in the Second Seminole War mirrored those of Jackson in the First Seminole War to a marked degree, there were two major differences. First, Scott's supply problem was based on difficulties of transportation rather than lack of the supplies themselves. Jackson had been unable to secure even basic provisions, while Scott found that the Commissary General of Subsistence had allocated adequate supplies in the depots, but that they could not be brought up to the forward troops for lack of transportation, roads, and maps. Second, Scott's plans were thrown awry by the intrusion of Gaines who, instead of confining his attention to the

An Indian chief, Emachitochustern, tried to avoid a second war. He wrote:

"I don't like to make any trouble or to have any quarrel with white people, but if they will trespass on my lands and rights, I must defend myself the best way I can."

He sent a letter on behalf of ten Seminole villages describing the Seminole's plight.

To the Commanding Officer at Fort Hawkins.
DEAR SIR:

"Since the last war, after you sent us word that we must quit the war, our red people have come over on this side. The white people have carried all the red people's cattle off. Bernard's son was here, and I asked him what to do about it - he told me to go to the head white man and complain. I did so, and there was no head white man, and there was no law in the case. *The whites first began to steal from us*, and there's nothing said about that, but great complaints about what the Indians do. It is now three years since white people killed three Indians; and since, they have killed three more; and since, one more. *The white people killed our red people first* - the Indians took satisfaction. There are three men that the red people have not taken satisfaction for yet. There is nothing said about what white people do - but all that the Indians do is brought up. The cattle that we are accused of taking, were cattle that the *white people took from us* - our young men went out and brought them back with the *same marks* and *brands*."

Far left: Brigadier General Zachary Taylor used bloodhounds to track down the Seminoles. Even though it was not effective, the practice caused considerable anger (especially in the middle and northern states) and was soon ended.
Below: Osceola was captured in November 1837 after he had been lured to a parley with American officers. The Seminole leader was imprisoned in Fort Moultrie, near Charleston, South Carolina, and died in the following year. The attending physician was Dr. Weedon, who then removed and preserved Osceola's head.

Rawson Clarke was one of three survivors from the Seminole attack on Major Dade's command, which took place in December 1835. Dade's column comprised 112 soldiers.

"It was 8 o'clock. Suddenly I heard a rifle shot in the direction of the advanced guard, and this was immediately followed by a musket shot from that quarter. Captain Fraser had rode by me a moment before in that direction. I never saw him afterwards. I had not time to think of the meaning of these shots, before a volley, as if from a thousand rifles, was poured in upon us from the front, and all along our left flank. I looked around me, and it seemed as if I was the only one left standing in the right wing. Neither could I, until several other vollies had been fired at us, see an enemy - and when I did, I could only see their heads and arms peering out from the long grass, far and near and from behind the pine trees. The first fire of the Indians was the most destructive, seemingly killing or disabling half our men.

We promptly threw ourselves behind trees, and opened a sharp fire of musketry. I, for one, never fired without seeing my man, that is, his head and shoulders … the Indians chiefly fired lying or squatting in the grass. Lt. Bassinger fired five or six rounds of cannister from the cannon. This appeared to frighten the Indians, and they retreated. We immediately began to fell trees, and erect a little triangular breastwork. Some of us went forward to gather the cartridge boxes from the dead, and to assist the wounded. I had seen Major Dade fall to the ground by the first volley. Whilst gathering the cartridges, I saw Lt. Mudge sitting his back reclining against a tree … his head fallen, and evidently dying. I spoke to him, but he did not answer.

We had barely raised our breastwork knee high, when we saw the Indians advancing in great numbers over the hill to our left. They came on boldly till within a long musket shot, when they spread themselves from tree to tree to surround us.

"Our men were by degrees all cut down. We had maintained a steady fight from 8 until 2 P.M. or thereabouts, and allowing three quarters of an hour interval between the first and second attack, had been pretty busily engaged for more than 5 hours. Lieut. B. was the only officer left alive, and he severely wounded. He told me as the Indians approached to lay down and feign myself dead. I looked through the logs, and saw the savages approaching in great numbers. A heavy made Indian, of middle stature, painted down to the waist, seemed to be the Chief. He made them a speech, frequently pointing to the breastwork. At length they charged into the work; there was none to offer resistance, and they did not seem to suspect the wounded being alive - offering no indignity, but stepping about carefully, quietly stripping off our accoutrements, and carrying away our arms. They then retired in a body in the direction from whence they came.

"Immediately upon their retreat, forty or fifty negroes on horseback galloped up and alighted, tied their beasts, and commenced with horrid shouts and yells the butchery of the wounded, together with an indiscrimate plunder, stripping the bodies of the dead of clothing, watches and money, and splitting open the heads of all who showed the least sign of life, with their axes and knives, and accompanying their bloody work with obscene and taunting derisions and with frequent cries of "what have you got to sell."

"Lieut. B. hearing the negroes butchering the wounded at length sprang up, and asked them to spare his life. They met him with the blows of their axes, and their fiendish laughter. Having been wounded in five different places myself, I was pretty well covered with blood, and two scratches that I had received on my head, gave to me the appearance of having been shot through the brain, for the negroes, after catching me up by the heels, threw me down saying "d….n him, he's dead enough!" They then stripped me of my clothes, shoes and hat, and left me."

In 1835 Frances and Almina Hall were captured by Indians. Their abduction caused considerable consternation all over the country for a while, but they eventually managed to escape.

Louisiana frontier with Mexico as ordered, arrived in Tampa Bay by sea with a large force of Louisiana militiamen. Gaines fed his men the supplies intended for Scott's command and then, after an inconclusive action against the Indians, returned to New Orleans during March. To add insult to injury, Gaines reported the action as a victory and thereby caused a reduction in the flow of supplies to Scott, who was now thought to be involved in a simple mopping-up operation after Gaines' "victory."

In St. Augustine, Scott began planning a new offensive under adverse conditions: for he had severely antagonized his volunteers and also the settlers of Florida with a suggestion of cowardice in an official request for 3,000 "good troops (not volunteers)." Florida settlers happily burned an effigy of Scott, and many cheered at the end of May when Scott was transferred to Georgia to suppress a Creek uprising that had started in eastern Alabama, but then threatened Georgia and Florida. In Georgia, Scott fell foul of the local commander, Brevet Major General Thomas S. Jesup, who had put down the Indian uprising in a decisive manner before Scott could complete and put into action his own, more complex, plan of campaign. Jesup felt that Scott had been too slow to plan and to act, and

informed Washington of the fact in no uncertain terms.

The upshot of the matter was an order for Scott to return to Washington, where he faced a court of inquiry. Scott was cleared by the court of any blame for the failure of the first Florida campaign, but was not returned to command in Florida. Instead, the general was employed on a number of sensitive diplomatic missions, in which he proved remarkably successful. Typical of these missions were the "Caroline Incident," the Arrowstook "War," and the Cherokee problem. The first was caused by the seizure on December 29, 1837, of the steamboat *Caroline* on the Niagara River by Canadian militia inside the United States. In the strict sense of the word, the Canadians had "invaded" the United States, and troops were concentrated along the border. Scott's diplomatic skills were used to good effect, however, and the possibility of war between the United States and the United Kingdom was removed. Then, in February 1838, the Arrowstook "War" occurred, when a dispute between Maine and New Brunswick about the incursion of Canadian loggers into American territory again threatened war. Scott's intervention eased tensions again, and the problem was removed by the Webster-Ashburton

Treaty of 1842, which settled the disputed frontier in this region between the United States and Canada. Scott's diplomacy was also instrumental in persuading 15,000 Cherokees to vacate Georgia and move peacefully to the west.

Meanwhile, the Second Seminole War continued in Florida. Jesup commanded from late 1836 until he was replaced in May 1838 by Brevet Brigadier General Zachary Taylor. Taylor was in turn relieved at his own request and replaced by Brevet Brigadier General Walker K. Armistead until May 1841, when the forceful Colonel William J. Worth was given the command by an exasperated Department of War.

The Battle of Lake Okeechobee

The sole decisive action of the war was the Battle of Lake Okeechobee, fought on December 25, 1837. About 1,000 Americans, consisting of about 500 regulars and 500 volunteers under Taylor's command, moved against the main Seminole position through the swamps. In the last two miles of the advance, Taylor arranged his force as two lines, with the volunteers in the first line. The volunteers broke against the Seminole defense, just as Taylor had reckoned. The American regulars were then able to smash forward against an Indian force already disorganized by the attack of the volunteers and sweep all before them. The Seminoles lost about half their effective strength, while the American losses were 26 killed and 112 wounded. Organized Seminole resistance was broken by the battle, but the will to resist was not seriously dented, and the war dragged on for almost six more years.

The war was fought on a desultory basis, with the Indians fighting a guerrilla campaign and the American side responding with a mixture of armed strength and attempted negotiation. Jesup was neither able to drive the Indians from the swamps nor to persuade them to leave Florida. The tactic devised by Taylor was the division of the Indians' area into small districts that were then sealed off individually and searched with the aid of bloodhounds. This search-and-destroy system might have worked in the long run, but the use of the dogs attracted severe criticism from all

This lithograph was published during 1837 in Charleston, South Carolina. The fury of this attack on an American fort is an indication of the general feeling in the south against the Seminoles.

U.S. Army, 7th Infantry, First Sergeant, 1835

For many years, the 7th Infantry was the garrison of Fort Gibson, on the Arkansas River in what is now Oklahoma. The fort was created by the regiment in 1824, when the commanding officer was Colonel Matthew Arbuckle. The soldier illustrated is a first sergeant, as indicated by his epaulets and sash; that he had served for more than ten years is shown by the chevrons on his sleeve. He wears an undress jacket (replaced on parade by a dark blue tailcoat). The cloth fatigue cap is fitted with a ''poke'' (visor).

quarters of American public opinion. The Department of War ordered Taylor to cease hostilities and try again to secure a negotiated settlement, but the only result was a sharp increase in Indian raids. Armistead also believed in negotiation, but he, too, failed to make any significant impact on the course of the war.

It was Worth who brought matters to an end. Previous commanders had not campaigned during the summer months for fear of fevers and dysentery. This respite had consistently allowed the Indians to plant, raise, and gather a harvest that maintained them through the following winter's campaigning season. Worth decided that the best way to defeat the Seminoles was to destroy their ability to sustain themselves. Throughout the summer of 1841, U.S. forces remained in the field, or rather the swamplands, with the intention of harassing the Indians and engaging all that they could trap, but more important, destroying their crops and their villages. The results fully justified Worth's reasoning, for increasing numbers of Indians emerged from the swamps into captivity and movement to the west. The Second Seminole War was declared officially ended in August 1842. In all, about 3,800 Seminoles were moved west over the "Trail of Tears," but the Second Seminole War had cost the army 1,600 dead, including a large number who had succumbed to disease. The war had involved a total of 10,000 regulars and 30,000 volunteers, and the strain imposed on the army was so great that, in July 1838, its authorized strength was increased from about 7,000 to 12,500 men.

Indian warriors attack Fort Mackenzie in the period 1840-1843.

Right: The removal of the southern Indian tribes toward Oklahoma resulted mainly from the political influence of white planters who wanted their lands, and the route of the displaced Indians became known as the "Trail of Tears." The tribes involved included the Cherokee, Chickasaw, Choctaw, Creek, and Seminole. The task of eviction and escort fell to the army, and this painting by Robert Lindneux emphasizes that the Indians were allowed to take relatively little with them, often leaving behind prosperous farms.

Below right: Another celebrated Seminole leader was Mito Chlucco, or "The Long Warrior."

Riverine Experience

The war was clearly not the type for which the army had been intended, trained, and equipped. As a result, the army acquired important experience in fighting a sustained war against irregular forces, and equally important, it improved its transportation system. River crossings were made easier by the adoption of a light pontoon wagon designed by the Quartermaster General's Department with a lining of rubberized fabric to make it waterproof and therefore buoyant. At the instigation of Jesup, the Corps of Artificers, disbanded after the War of 1812, was revived, and the corps' mechanics and skilled workmen soon became vital in the all-important task of keeping wagons and boats serviceable. The Second Seminole War also taught the army much about the usefulness and nature of water transportation. Until then, the army had hired civilian steamboats when necessary, but now turned increasingly toward the creation of its own fleet, which proved far more efficient and ultimately cheaper.

Army Exploration Teams in the West

Throughout this period, but on the other side of the United States, the army had been sending out expeditions toward the

western coast of North America. During the 1820s and 1830s, the smallest of these expeditions had been concerned mainly with exploration, while larger efforts were undertaken with the aim of protecting trade caravans and contacting and establishing friendly relations with the Indian tribes of the Great Plains. In the 1840s, the emphasis shifted rapidly toward protection and support of the settlers who were sweeping into the newly opened west. This new wave of settlement spurred further exploration; typical were the two expeditions headed by 2nd Lieutenant John C. Fremont of the Corps of Topographical Engineers. The 1842 party explored and mapped the area around the upper reaches of the Platte River to ease the task of settlers pushing northwest along the Oregon Trail. The 1843 party pushed across the Rocky Mountains to explore much of northern California. Reports from such expeditions also help to give an indication of how rapidly the wave of expansion was growing. The 1842 Fremont expedition, for example, reported seeing settlers totaling 64 men and 16 or 17 parties. Just three years later, Colonel Stephen W. Kearny and five companies of the 1st Dragoon Regiment traveled along the Oregon Trail for the protection of settlers, and reported 850 men and about 475 parties grouped into wagon trains with thousands of cattle.

However, the majority of settlers were not heading west into northern California, but were moving southwest toward Texas, then in northeastern Mexico. After an early experiment under the Spanish regime, Texas was formally opened to American immigration in 1823. It is estimated that in the period 1825-30 about 15,000 American citizens and several thousand slaves poured into the region in response to the Mexican government's offer of land grants and the promise of a fair legal system. Matters did not develop as the American immigrants, who soon came to call themselves Texans, had hoped. The American community in Texas grew away from the Mexican community as the Texans tried to create an American way of life for themselves. The Mexicans became increasingly worried that Texas was becoming too Americanized and sought to impose full Mexican control. At the same time, the Mexican garrisons in Texas were strengthened. The Texans saw both these factors as evidence of political repression, and this feeling was strengthened when a ban on further American immigration was imposed in April 1830. Immigration continued without much difficulty, however, and by 1835 there were about 28,000 Americans in Texas.

American dealings with the Indians were not all as unhappy as those with the southern tribes. This illustration shows "Camp Comanche," a trading establishment based on a wagon train, in 1844.

The Seminole Wars featured booby traps and ambushes, a type of combat much like that which a later American army experienced in Vietnam. An artillerist, Randolf Ridgely, provided the latest Indian news in a letter to a relative dated 4 March, 1840.

We have a little Indian news lately. Capt. Rains 7th. Infantry placed a shell on an Indian trail and covered it with a shirt. An Indian came and removed the shirt when the shell exploded and wounded him severely. Capt. R. then put 4 shells in a blanket and placed them on another trail. The Indians discovered and resolved to catch him in his own trap. So they collected their warriors to the number of 85 or 90 surrounded the spot; they then by means of a cord exploded the shell - down goes Capt. R. with a Sergt. Corpl. and 16 men - on coming to the place he found an old "Koon" dead - whilst he was kicking or turning the Koon over with his foot the Indians rose up and fired. The men behaved very handsomely, at once formed and extended. The Chief of the party was twice seen to step out and fire at the Sergt. who was very active in forming his men. The third time he struck the Sergt. when he (the sergt.) turned and rushed at the Indian until he got to pretty close quarters, he then fired and killed the rascal. When their chief fell the Indians fell back and slackened their fire considerably - in the mean time Capt. Rains had been shot down. The Sergt. seeing the effect produced on the enemy charged them boldly then rapidly retreated and thus succeeded in getting clear with Capt. R. and other wounded men. We had two killed, Capt. R. and 4 others wounded; the former mortally being shot through the lungs. They were separated at the commencement and could not join the party on account of the Indians being between them lay concealed - one says he counted 91 and the other says 93 Indians. The Indians lost their chief Halie-Tuskinuger and three others. The chief was in at Tampa last summer and boasted he could in two days bring into the field 80 warriors. As he had 4 or 5 days to collect them it is thought they are very little if any over rated. I heard Major McClintock and Capt. Gainor speak of this man two months ago; both agreed they considered him the most cunning, smart, hostile Indian they had yet seen in Florida.

Capt. Holmes also got on a trail of Indians and after following it for two days, he thought they were doging him and accordingly made a Sergt. and a few men conceal themselves, he had passed but a short time when two Indians came up with their rifles, the party killed one and captured the other. Holmes continued on, and captured 14 ponies. This is all the Indian news. It is thought by many Genl. Armistead will be in command, he is expecting orders daily as Macomb told him he would certainly have command he is now in St Augustine as also Col. Walback, Major Payne - and others being on a Court for trial of Capt. Howe - but the Court decided as the specification embraced man slaughter they would not try him. I write in the utmost haste as it is sun down and the boat leaves St. Augustine at Sun rise. Best regards to Drs. Baldwin, Tallifers, McLaughlin, Murray, Winder, Lese. I have had the tallest kind of fun in town lately

Your friend
RANDOLPH RIDGELY W.A. Carter Esq.
Key Biscayne.

I believe the Regt. will go out this summer."

Major George McCall describes the pursuit of the Seminoles through the Big Cypress Swamp. The chase began on December 14, 1841.

The next morning I took forty men of my company for an exploring party. I steered south, and after wading about two miles, came in sight of a live oak hummock, for this I steered, and soon saw signs of Indians.

Through many parts of the Cypress here, there grows in the water a long grass, which, when pressed down by a person in passing, does not rise again, and thus leaves a very plain trail. I followed this trail for some miles, when it led me to a small wet prairie. Here the party had separated for the purpose of leaving no trail on ground comparatively dry; but the guide soon found and pointed out to me the foot-prints of six men and one woman who had walked here abreast and about three yards apart. After some time I came to another and larger prairie, alternately dry and wet, having on the east in the distance a large live-oak hummock, on the south a formidable cypress, and on the west strips of pine woods. Here we pressed hot upon the trail, and the guide expressed his belief that the Prophet could not be many miles off, judging from the appearance of the country. But we had not gone far before the guide discovered that they had been playing a deep game, which is managed in this way: - When they wish to conceal their abode, their approach to it is never direct, and perhaps often leading you by a plain trail past it; the foremost of the party will, by making a high, long step over the top of the grass to the right or left, light upon the toe only, and step by step carefully arranging the grass thus disturbed, make his escape; his absence will scarcely be observed upon the trail, and the one who succeeds him as leader, pursues the route for some hundred yards, then he makes his escape in like manner; and so on, till but one is left, and he also continues the direct course, till deep water, a thicket, a rock, or something of the kind, affords him also an opportunity to escape, and the most skilful in this accomplishment brings up the rear.

This game was successfully played in this case, the last one being a man with a very large foot (for an Indian). He led us to deep pond, where among the rocks he gave the slip to all pursuers. We searched around the pond, but could not discover a trace of where he had left it.

It is thought, however, the Indians are somewhere down there still; and as we expect a supply of rations to-morrow, we shall set out with as much as we can properly carry, and penetrate, if possible, to the end of the land.

But the Army continued its relentless chase.

The Indians having been driven from the south and east, had (some of them) sought refuge in the scrubs and hummocks around Is-tok-po-ga Lake, and thither we marches. We were now, however, entering a country in which horses could be used, and from that time I had one at my command. But the idea of catching Indians even here was looked upon as perfectly ridiculous. They have become wilder and more vigilant than the beasts of the forest, and show more caution and sagacity in moving and concealing their wives and children than does the wild deer towards her fawn. A wiser and more humane policy was adopted; the troops were marched to the vicinity of the district known to be their abode, and then some friendly Indians were induced by heavy bribes to venture forward to endeavor by persuasion and large promises to induce them to come in; at the same time to assure them that the troops would continue the chase to the very last, in case of refusal.

The hour was propitious; they were found much harassed and broken down in spirit and in body. The women, who throughout the war have displayed more than Spartan heroism, now wept and implored their husbands to yield to the entreaties of the envoys. Three days and sleepless nights were passed in combating the resolution never to leave Florida. But the ladies at length (as is always the case) prevailed, and Assinoah, the chief, consented to come in.

U.S. Army, New England Guards, Color-Bearer, 1840

Quite separate from the regular army and the common militia were the units of chartered State Volunteers. In name, these units were part of the militia organization; but in practice they were independent (and indeed almost private) units that formed a distinct part of the social system of most eastern cities. The man illustrated is a member of the celebrated New England Guards, located in Boston, Massachusetts. The blue uniform and tall shako complete with heavy brass plate and cock's feathers are typical of Volunteer style of the period, and the standard bears the arms of the State of Massachusetts.

The Texas Revolution (1835-36)

In June 1832, some Texans fought a brief skirmish with Mexican troops at Velasco. This encounter persuaded most Texans that something had to be done about the situation, and a convention was held at San Felipe. The convention prepared a formal request for Texan autonomy within Mexico, which would involve an administrative separation of Texas from the province of Coahuila and increased representation by Texans in the Mexican congress. The leader of the Texas faction demanding greater autonomy for Texas within Mexico was Steven Austin, whose father had emigrated from Missouri in 1811. A smaller faction, which wanted complete independence, was growing all the time. In December 1832, Sam Houston crossed the Red River into Texas, and soon became a leader in the independence party. Houston was an extremely colorful character, an ex-general of the militia, a governor of Tennessee, a friend of Andrew Jackson, an experienced sol-

"Sam" Houston, the architect of Texas independence, ultimately guaranteed that independence with his victory over the Mexicans in the Battle of San Jacinto.

Right: Frontier operations demanded considerable flexibility in uniform and equipment. In general terms, those units which displayed the greatest flexibility enjoyed the highest success. These are weapons typical of frontier warfare, including a fighting axe, a European dagger, and two fighting knives.

Steven Austin
For further references see pages
121,123,124

Sam Houston
For further references see pages
67,124,125,126, 128,129,130, *131*

dier who had been wounded twice in the Creek wars, and an adopted Cherokee.

In April 1833, the Texans held a second convention to demand greater self-government, and as a result, Austin was thrown into jail. Dislike of the dictatorial regime headed by General Antonio Lopez de Santa Anna was growing throughout Mexico during this period. During the first half of the 1830s, there were rebellions in eight Mexican states. Santa Anna crushed an uprising in Zacatecas during April 1835, and he sent General Martin

Perfecto de Cos, his brother-in-law, to deal with the rebellion in Coahuila. In June 1835, the Texans learned from Mexican dispatches that civil rights were about to be suspended in Texas, and that Santa Anna was planning to tackle the Texans personally. This produced a further increase in strength for what had now become the Texas "war party." One of the leaders of this faction was William Barret Travers, a hothead who had previously been a lawyer in South Carolina. At his instigation, the garrison

Santa Anna
For further references see pages
122,123,*124*,125,126, 127,128,130,*131*

THE WAR OF TEXAS REVOLUTION

MILES 0 — 100
KILOMETERS 0 — 150

UNITED STATES

UNITED STATES

Occupied by Gaines
July - Dec 1836

Louisiana

Nacogdoches

Brazos River

Trinity River

Sabine River

Houston begins
withdrawal east,
pursued by Santa Anna.
May 11, 1836

Texas proclaims
Independence
March 2, 1836

San Jacinto River

Washington-
on-the-Brazos

Bastrop

Lynchburg

SAN JACINTO

Harrisburg

New Washington

ALAMO

Gonzales

Colorado River

Cos surrenders to
Texans under Burleson.
Dec 9, 1835

Guadalupe River

TEXAS

San Antonio River

Presido De
Rio Grande

Santa Anna leaves Mexico City
Nov. 28, 1835
Crosses Rio Grande
Feb. 12, 1836
Arrives in San Antonio
Feb. 23, 1836

Nuecees River

La Bahia

Refugio

GULF OF MEXICO

Republic of Texas / Mexico
boundary.
March 1836 - Feb. 1846

Rio Grande

Mexico boundary
from July 1848

M E X I C O

Matamoros

THE BATTLE OF SAN JACINTO

Texan Force
600 men
(Houston)

1 Regt.
(Burleson)

2 Regt.
(Sherman)

Artillery
(Hockley)

Regulars
(Millard)

Infantry

Cavalry
(Lamar)

Infantry

Cavalry

Reserves

Prairie

Mexican Army
1,250 men
(Santa Anna)

Peggy Lake

Texans advance
1630 hrs. April 21, 1836
Battle lasts 18 minutes
600 Mexicans Killed

was ejected from the Mexican customs post at Anahuac. Even as Cos began to move Mexican forces into Texas, most Texans still wanted peace. However, this feeling was swayed toward war when a much-changed Austin was released from jail and declared both that Santa Anna was a "base, unprincipled bloody monster" and that "War is our only recourse. No halfway measures, but war in full."

The result was open rebellion. In October 1835, a detachment of Mexican troops was sent to recover a virtually useless cannon which had been lent to the citizens of Gonzales in 1831 to frighten the Indians. The Texans hung a banner underneath the cannon, with the legend "Come and Take It." On October 2, the Texas Revolution started when a force of Texans fired on the Mexican detachment, killing one man and putting the rest to flight.

In San Antonio, there was a Mexican strength of 1,400 under Cos. The quality of the force was low, for Santa Anna had sent to Texas what were in effect penal regiments manned almost entirely by criminals. About 500 Texans had gathered at Gonzales. Most were undisciplined farmers, but there were enough

Far left: The War of Texas Revolution.
Above left: The Battle of San Jacinto.
Left: The Siege of the Alamo.
Below: The Alamo.

THE SIEGE OF THE ALAMO

Santa Anna begins
bombardment
Feb 24, 1836

San Antonio

SAN
ANTONIO

ALAMO

MEXICAN
BATTERIES

La Villita

2

3

6

1

4

5

THE ALAMO

North Gate

Breach

Ditch

Plaza

The
Alamo

Cattle
Pen

Corral

Hospital

Church

South
Gate

Palisades

0500 hrs., March 6
3,000 Mexicans in final
assault against
183 Texans

0630 hrs.
183 Texans and
600 Mexicans dead

0   100
FEET

frontiersmen with rifles to give the Texas force some military capability. Austin was elected commander, despite his lack of military skills, and given the authority to prevent the men from coming and going as they pleased. A local command was voted to Houston, who then headed for the Texas convention at San Felipe.

"Democracy" Runs Riot

The Texas "army" now told Austin that it wanted to attack San Antonio, and the democratically elected commander was forced to agree, even though strength had fallen to only 300. On October 27 at Concepcion Mission, about two miles south of San Antonio, a Mexican detachment was severely handled by a much smaller party of Texans, led by James Bowie, the celebrated knife duelist and landowner. The Texans lost just one man killed, but the Mexicans lost 67 dead and about the same number wounded by the Texans' long-range but accurate rifle fire. Despite Bowie's success, the Texans were in no position to attack San Antonio and therefore laid siege to the town.

The Texas convention opened on November 3. All agreed that the Texans'

General Antonio Lopez de Santa Anna proved unequal to the task of maintaining a Mexican grasp on Texas during the Texas Revolution. Despite his defeat in the Battle of San Jacinto, he harbored the belief that he would be able to reverse the decision of the war.

war against Santa Anna's dictatorship had to be continued. While some argued in favor of the cause of independence, others wanted to fight in the name of the Mexican federal state. Houston was a supporter of the latter idea, which was adopted by the convention with the suggestion that Texas offer to help any other Mexican state wishing to throw off Santa Anna's shackles. Austin was sent to the United States to seek help, and command of the army passed to Edward Burleson.

There was considerable, although not total, public support in the United States for the Texans. Weapons and other supplies began to flood across the frontier into Texas, and volunteer companies were organized, most of them in the south. The United States decided not to participate, and strict instructions were issued to General Gaines to maintain a neutral zone along the Sabine River. Part of this order covered Gaines' responsibility in preventing Indian raids from American territory into Mexico, but Gaines understood this as meaning that there should be no conflict of American and Mexican interests. He therefore sent the 7th Infantry Regiment and part of the 1st Dragoon Regiment to Nacogdoches in July 1836, withdrawing them from this illegal excursion into Mexico only in December.

In Texas, the dividing line between the factions for and against independence from Mexico was becoming more defined, and so too was that between the Tejanos, inhabitants of Mexican descent. Meanwhile, the "siege" of San Antonio was progressing in an extraordinary way, for the democracy of the Texan "army" meant that all decisions were reached only by a majority vote of the officers, and the men came and went as they pleased. With the approach of winter, the volunteers began to depart in larger numbers, and a majority vote of the officers overruled Burleson and decided to break off the siege.

Despite the strength of the Mexican defense of San Antonio, with the garrison holding well-prepared positions, the volunteers from the United States had other ideas. Led by Ben Milam, a Kentuckian who had fought for Mexican independence and only recently escaped from the Mexican jail into which he had been thrown for his republican notions, 300 Texans and volunteers stormed into San Antonio on December 5. With two companies of American volunteers, the New Orleans Grays, in the lead, the Texans took San Antonio in four days of hand-to-hand fighting. Milam was killed by a sharpshooter, but Cos offered to surrender on December 9. Burleson accepted the offer and sent the Mexicans home with enough weapons to fight off Indian attack.

With such a victory under their belts, the Texans thought that the war was all but over and departed for home in large numbers. Houston was convinced that this was not the case, but his appeal for the men to remain under arms went unheeded. Texas strength was then reduced further by an unfathomable decision of some Texans to take Matamoros at the mouth of the Rio Grande. Those who departed toward Matamoros offered the reason that they would link up with the local anti-Santa Anna faction and start a Mexican war

The boat carronade was one of several types produced to give light vessels a devastating punch in short-range engagements. Such weapons were usually mounted in the bow of a boat: if it was mounted as a broadside gun, its recoil could have damaged the boat's structure or, under certain circumstances, even overturned it.

to overthrow Santa Anna. Houston was strongly against the expedition, which was nonetheless approved by the convention in San Felipe and dispatched under James Fannin, whose initial move was to secure a base at La Bahia. The Texas head of state, Governor Henry Smith, agreed with Houston and dismissed the council until March 1, 1836, when it was to reassemble at Washington-on-the-Brazos. The council responded by dismissing Smith as "vulgar and depraved." Houston argued with the men of the Matamoros· expedition that the defense of Texas was more important, and by the time the expedition left La Bahia under Colonel Frank Johnson, it numbered just 70 men, who were massacred when they tried to execute the ill-conceived scheme.

The Undermanned Alamo

This division left just 104 men under Colonel James C. Neill to hold the Alamo, a fort improvised out of a mission station just east of San Antonio. The defenses were put in order by Green Jameson, and 18 of the cannon abandoned by the Mexicans were remounted and placed on earthwork ramparts inside and outside the 12-foot wall surrounding the compound.

Meanwhile, Santa Anna had been putting the finishing touches on his plan to keep Texas as part of Mexico. Early in 1836, Santa Anna's Army of Operations in Texas had about 6,000 men, a figure that had increased to about 7,500 by mid-April. Houston correctly saw that a pitched battle against this force of regulars and militia, regardless of its failings in equipment and discipline, would result in a defeat for the Texans. He therefore planned to concentrate and train his forces while fighting a guerrilla war that would cost Mexican lives and overtax their lines of communication. Only when the Mexican force had dwindled in numbers and capability would the Texan commander consider a formal battle. As part of this overall plan, Houston detached Bowie with 30 men to destroy the fortifications of the Alamo and bring out the garrison.

Arriving at the Alamo, Houston found

This watercolor by Shegogue, painted in 1831, reveals David Crockett the congressman, rather than Davy Crockett, the backwoodsman and hero of the Alamo.

that Neill's strength was down to 80 men. The others had returned home for lack of pay and supplies. Bowie and Neill then decided to hold the Alamo because they lacked the means to evacuate the cannons, and the remaining men were prepared to hold this fort on Santa Anna's inevitable northward march against Texas. Houston was again appalled, for first Fannin and now Neill and Bowie had disobeyed his orders. He tried to resign, but Governor Brown instead gave him leave until March 1. Houston departed on a mission to guarantee the neutrality of the Cherokees.

On February 1, Santa Anna left Saltillo at the head of his army, which was made up of two infantry brigades, one cavalry brigade, some artillery, and a crack engineer corps. At the Rio Grande, he planned to link up with a force already there under General Joaquin Sesma, while a small detachment under General Jose Urrea headed for Matamoros. Almost immediately, the deficiencies of the

Mexican supply system became clear. The march toward Texas became a feat of endurance as the starving men and animals moved through the dust of the lower areas and the snows of the mountains. The men were already on half rations when the army was hit by cholera, which swept through the already weakened ranks and killed many men.

The situation at the Alamo was improving slightly at this time. Bowie had used his contacts with the local population to get supplies, and as the defenses were put in order, a trickle of reinforcements arrived in response to Bowie's claim that "We cannot be driven from the post of honor." On February 3, Lieutenant Colonel William B. Travis appeared with 30 men, and five days later, "Colonel" David Crockett arrived with his Tennessee Company of Mounted Volunteers. Already famous as an Indian fighter, ex-Congressman, and storyteller, "Davy" Crockett announced that he had come with his small company "to aid you all that I can

The siege of the Alamo ended on March 6, 1836, when the Mexican forces launched their final assault on the vastly outgunned Texas position and its outnumbered garrison.

in your noble cause." By February 10, the garrison of the Alamo numbered 142 men, and Neill went on leave after giving command to Travis. This appointment did not meet with the approval of most of the volunteers, but as Bowie was in poor health and in any event was generally absent on drunken rampages in San Antonio, the decision was probably right. On February 14, Travis and Bowie settled the matter by agreeing to a joint command.

The Siege of the Alamo Begins

Just two days later, Santa Anna crossed the Rio Grande after linking up with Sesma's force at Presidio de Rio Grande. Final preparations were being completed in the Alamo with the creation of a hospital, the chopping of horseshoes into grapeshot, and the finding of accommodations for the families of several volunteers. Travis sent out requests for reinforcement, most of them aimed at Fannin, who was now settled in "Fort Defiance" at La Bahia.

Santa Anna's army arrived in San Antonio on February 23, about one month earlier than the Texans had anticipated. The men of the Alamo's garrison in San Antonio quickly pulled east across the San Antonio River and reached the Alamo, which now contained about 25 women and children in addition to about 150 men. Travis had time to send out a batch of appeals for reinforcement, again to Fannin and another to Gonzales, about 70 miles away, which was at the time the nearest point from which help could have been expected. Santa Anna set about besieging the Texas garrison with no delay. He even hoisted on the belfry of the church in San Antonio a red flag signifying that no quarter would be given.

Within a day, the Alamo was firmly under Mexican siege, and on February 24, Santa Anna's artillery opened up a bombardment of the fort. On the same day, Bowie's poor health finally caught up with him, and he took to his bed, leaving Travis in sole command. Another message was sent out by Travis: "..our flag still waves proudly from the walls - I shall never surrender or retreat. Then, I call on you in the name of Liberty, of patriotism & everything dear to the American character, to come to our aid...if this call is neglected, I am determined to sustain myself as long as possible & die like a soldier who never forgets what is due to his honor & that of his country - Victory or Death."

The next day, the Tennessee volunteers raided and burned the shacks south of the Alamo used by the Mexicans as advanced positions for the concealment of sharpshooters. Effective artillery support for the raid was supplied by the Texas artillery under the control of Captain Almeron Dickinson and Captain William Carey. Another message was sent out by Travis, this time carried by Captain Juan Seguin, whose San Antonio company of Tejanos formed part of the garrison. In this message, Travis wrote that "It will be impossible for us to keep them out much longer. If they overpower us, we fall a sacrifice at the shrine of our

country, and we hope posterity will do our memory justice. Give me help, oh my Country!"

Fannin was at last stirred to action of a sort. On February 26, he left La Bahia for the Alamo, though he halted for a day when a wagon broke down only a few hundred yards along the road. Then on February 27, Fannin retired to La Bahia once more. Some help was forthcoming, however, for at Gonzales the 25 men of Lieutenant George Kimball's Gonzales Ranging Company of Mounted Volunteers decided to assist the garrison of the Alamo. In the early morning of February 29, they slipped through the Mexican lines to reach the Alamo.

It was too late for further assistance to reach the Alamo, but Travis' patriotic pleas finally spurred the Texas convention into action. Reconvened at Washington-on-the-Brazos, the convention declared Texas an independent nation on March 2. Fannin again decided to move in support of the Alamo, with the intention of joining forces with the volunteers that Seguin was rallying for a relief attempt. Yet again, however, Fannin changed his mind.

The Fall of the Alamo

The Alamo had been under fairly constant artillery bombardment that had knocked down large parts of the walls. On March 5, Santa Anna decided that the time was ripe for an assault: some of his artillery had pushed to within 250 yards of the Alamo, and he had been reinforced with another brigade to give him an effective strength of more than 2,000 men. The assault was committed on March 6, and the fort was attacked by four columns of Mexicans starting at 5a.m. By 6:30a.m., it was all over, and the defenders of the Alamo were all dead with the exception of a few women and children, and one Tejano who persuaded the Mexicans he had been a prisoner. Mexican losses were about 600.

Houston arrived in Gonzales on March 11 and found 374 men gathered under Neill and Burleson for the relief of the Alamo. News of the Alamo's fall reached the Texans at Gonzales, and Houston decided to fall back in the face of Sesma's

The Alamo
For further references see pages 122, 123, 126, 127, 129

The death of Davy Crockett during the final Mexican assault on the Alamo.

advance on the town with 700 men. This retreat to the east was attacked by Houston's political opponents as the "Runaway Scrape." It was also unpopular with part of the Gonzales force, but was in fact very sensible as many of the men lacked weapons, and there were no supplies. The Texas government abandoned Washington-on-the-Brazos at the same time, finally establishing itself at Harrisburg under the newly elected provisional president, David Burnet.

The main Texas force was at La Bahia under Fannin. It was comparatively well trained and adequately equipped. The infantry units were the Georgia and Lafayette battalions, both created out of independent companies, and there was a small detachment of artillery. Fannin now proceeded to waste his force. A company under Captain King was sent to Refugio to evacuate its civilians, but was intercepted by Urrea's detachment and overrun. King and a few other survivors were tied to trees and shot. The Georgia battalion was then sent under Major Ward to find King's company and was also overrun. Reduced to a strength of 300 infantrymen and 25 cavalry, Fannin destroyed the fortifications of La Bahia, spiked the guns he could not move, and marched to join Houston.

The "Goliad Massacre"

Fannin's progress was slow, for his force was weighed down with baggage. Even though a move of only two more miles would have brought the force to the Rio Coleto and its timbered banks, Fannin camped in open countryside and was attacked by a superior Mexican force. Fannin formed his men into a hollow square with cannon in the corners and repulsed the first Mexican cavalry charge. Then, the Texans' rifles took a heavy toll of the Mexicans until the fall of night brought hostilities to a temporary end. On the following day, March 20, the Mexicans received reinforcement, including two cannon. Fannin's force was out of artillery ammunition, and the commander offered his men the opportunity to surrender or fight their way out. The Alabama Red Rovers wanted to fight, but because of their 70 wounded and the Mexicans' promise of fair treatment, the majority chose to surrender. Fannin's force returned to La Bahia under Mexican escort, where they found a number of other prisoners. On March 27, the majority of the Texans were marched out of La Bahia. Those who remained were mainly colonists from Refugio and San Patricio, medical staff, and a number of volunteers who had been captured while unarmed. The Mexicans said that the men being marched out were to be repatriated to the United States, but then opened fire. In this "Goliad Massacre," 342 of the prisoners were killed, and only about 30 escaped. The legal reason for the massacre was a Mexican law of 1835 which decreed the death penalty for all foreigners captured under arms in Texas.

This massacre left only Houston and his force to oppose Santa Anna's total control of Texas. Houston continued to fall back, but after crossing the Rio Brazos, halted and started to turn his force into a more disciplined army, with the 1st Regiment commanded by Burleson and the new 2nd Regiment by Sidney Sherman. Over the next two weeks, two cannon and some reinforcements arrived, giving Houston a strength of about 800 men including a mounted scouting troop under Captain H. Karnes. There was resentment at Houston's inaction, and nearly a mutiny when the threat of summary execution was used to

prevent the departure of a small force under Mirabeau Buonaparte Lamar in search of the Mexicans.

Santa Anna's Decisive Mistake

Houston was completely right, for Santa Anna finally committed the error for which the Texan commander was waiting. With his lines of communication completely overextended, Santa Anna sent General Gaona's division north from San Antonio, and General Urrea's division south from La Bahia toward Matagorda and Brazoria. He himself led 750 men of Sesma's division toward Fort Bend, where Sesma was to join him with the rest of the division. Santa Anna's main intention was to capture the members of the Texas government.

The Texas government avoided Santa Anna, who turned aside to find and destroy Houston. Santa Anna ordered the balance of his force at Fort Bend to meet him without delay, but in forced marches that covered 60 miles in just over two days, Houston and his Texas army approached Santa Anna before he had been reinforced. On April 20, Houston used his tactical advantage to cross Buffalo Bayou into a good defensive position offered by woods along the Rio San Jacinto. Cos arrived on April 21, bringing Santa Anna's strength to about 1,300 infantry, a few cavalry, and a single gun. Santa Anna located his force behind a barrier of supplies and pack saddles on the flat

ground in front of the Texans and waited for the attack. In the Texas ranks, there was the inevitable demand that Houston should order an attack. Houston said that the men should eat their midday meal first and sent a small party to destroy the bridge by which more reinforcements might reach Santa Anna.

The Texans then deployed, with the cavalry on the right flank, hidden from the Mexicans by the woods, and the 1st and 2nd Regiments on the left and right wings, with the Texans' two pieces of artillery between them. These guns, nicknamed "The Two Sisters," were gifts from the citizens of Cincinnati. The Mexicans clearly did not expect a battle to start so late in the day, and while Santa Anna slept in his tent, most of the Mexican force took its customary siesta in the field.

The Battle of San Jacinto

Houston started his advance at 4:30p.m. on April 21, and the Battle of San Jacinto was a complete rout of the Mexicans. The Texans got within 200 yards of the Mexican position without being noticed, and within 60 yards before the Mexicans had manned their positions and begun to fire. Santa Anna's flanks crumbled, allowing Lamar's cavalry to sweep around onto the Mexicans' left and Sherman's infantry to start passing around their right. The battle was over in just 18 minutes. Of the 783 Texans, two had been killed and 23 wounded, while the Mexicans had lost 600 dead and 730 taken prisoner. Santa Anna was captured on the following day as he tried to escape, but was not executed as Houston realized that the Mexican dictator was essential to any peace negotiations. Santa Anna recognized the independence of the Republic of Texas, although this recognition was later repudiated by the Mexican government. Houston was elected president, and on July 4 the United States recognized Texas. This move stirred considerable resentment in Mexico and contributed to sporadic border skirmishing between Texas and Mexico over the next ten years.

Santa Anna surrenders to Houston after the Battle of San Jacinto, and so brings the fighting in the Texas Revolution to an end.

Glossary

Adjutant General The professional head of the army department responsible for matters of personnel.

Arsenai A depot for the storage of military equipment (especially weapons and other munitions) for distribution in times of crisis or war.

Artillery An overall term for a tube weapon too large for operation by a single man. It is designed to fire solid shot or explosive-filled shell.

Battalion The basic organizational and tactical grouping, mainly of infantry, commanded by a lieutenant colonel and made up of several companies.

Battery The basic organizational and tactical grouping of artillery equivalent to an infantry company.

Blockade The closing up of a country or region to prevent entry or departure of people and goods.

Blockhouse A small fort, generally built of logs or other locally available materials, for local security along lines of communication and the like.

Brig A two-masted vessel with square sails on each mast.

Brigade The organizational and tactical grouping of two or more regiments, generally commanded by a brigadier general.

Brigantine A two-masted vessel with square sails on the foremast and fore- and-aft sails in the mainmast.

Canister An artillery-fired projectile for use against people, and generally made of a quantity of shot (the size of small cannon balls or large musket balls) in a thin metal container. The ''canister'' bursts open when it leaves the muzzle of the gun, allowing the shot to spread out into a large but even pattern.

Carriage The mobile or fixed support for piece of artillery, usually including the elevating and traversing mechanisms.

Cavalry The branch of any army intended to move and fight on horseback.

Company An organizational and tactical grouping, usually of infantry, commanded by a captain, and grouped to create a battalion.

Corvette A single-deck warship smaller than a frigate and generally used for scouting or, more frequently, raiding merchant shipping.

Demobilization The orderly disbandment of an army or other armed force at the end of hostilities.

Dragoon A cavalryman trained and equipped to fight as an infantryman if needed.

Establishment Any authorized strength of men, weapons, and equipment, seldom matched by actual numbers.

Fighting top A platform built at the top of a mast to support the shrouds stabilizing higher masts. In action, they were manned by marines and sailors with small arms, grenades, and on occasion light swivel guns to fire down onto an enemy ship's decks.

Flank The extreme left or right of a body of troops in a military position.

Frigate A single-deck ship of between 28 and 48 guns. It lacks the firepower and protection to take part in a fleet action, but has the speed and maneuverability to scout for line-of-battle ships and harass enemy shipping.

Galley A small warship relying on oars instead of sails as its main method of propulsion.

Garrison The unit or units attached to a base or other area for defense and the maintenance of its facilities.

Guerrilla Any man involved in irregular warfare waged by small parties operating independently, usually to harass the enemy's lines of communication, etc.

Howitzer A piece of artillery designed to fire at an angle of elevation higher than 45°. It lobs its shells high over any obstacle for a plunging descent on the target.

Infantry The branch of any army intended to move and fight on foot.

Inspector General The professional head of the army department responsible for training.

Light infantry Infantry equipped more lightly than infantry of the line, and thus able to march more quickly and to operate as skirmishers.

Line(s) of communication The main route(s) over which an army in the field is supplied, reinforced and provided with orders from a base area.

Magazine A storage area for gunpowder and/or other munitions.

Militia Citizen force with a commitment to annual training and, under specific conditions of geography and time, active service.

Musket A personal weapon (usually of the infantry) with a comparatively short but smooth-bored barrel that does not impart any spin to its bullet. It offers only modest accuracy and range, but gives a fairly rapid rate of fire.

Operational The adjective used to describe the level of military activity between the tactical and the strategic, and therefore concerned mainly with the coordination of battles to produce a campaign.

Ordnance The collective noun for artillery and its ammunition.

Quartermaster General The professional head of the army department responsible for supplies and accommodation.

Rampart A broad-topped mound of earth, usually with a stone parapet, for defensive purposes.

Regiment The basic organizational and tactical grouping commanded by a colonel and made up of two battalions.

Rifle A personal weapon (usually of the infantry) with a comparatively long barrel containing spiral internal grooves designed to spin the bullet. It provides high accuracy and long range, but only a low rate of fire.

Schooner A vessel with two or more masts each rigged with fore-and-aft sails.

Sharpshooter An individual soldier who is accurate enough (usually) with the rifle to be posted where marksmanship is needed.

Skirmisher A lightly equipped foot soldier deployed forward of the main body of troops to reconnoiter and harass the enemy's advance.

Sloop A small single-masted vessel rigged with fore-and-aft sails.

Spiking The act of rendering a piece of artillery useless, generally by hammering a spike into its touchhole.

Strategic The adjective used to describe the level of military activity above the operational, and therefore concerned mainly with coordination of campaigns to produce a war-winning situation.

Strike a flag To lower a naval flag in surrender

Tactical The adjective used to describe the level of military activity below the operational, and therefore concerned mainly with winning individual battles.

Topography The art of describing and representing on a map natural and artificial features of a geographical region.

Trail The leg connecting a gun carriage to its towing vehicle or animal. It is used to stabilize the weapon when it is deployed for action.

Bibliography

Baldwin, Leland D. *Whiskey Rebels, the Story of a Frontier Uprising.*
(University of Pittsburgh Press, Pittsburgh, PA, 1939).
The Whiskey Rebellion.

Bemrose, John. *Reminisces of the Second Seminole War.*
(University of Florida, Gainesville, FL, 1966).
Reprint of eyewitness account.

Buker, George E. *Swamp Sailors: Riverine Warfare in the Everglades 1835-1842.*
(University of Florida, Gainesville, Fl, 1975).
Seminole wars.

de la Pena, Jose Enrique. *With Santa Anna in Texas.*
(Texas A & M University Press, College Station, TX, 1975).
Diary of the period.

Downey, Fairfax. *Indian Wars of the U.S. Army 1776-1865.*
(Doubleday & Co, Garden City, NY, 1963).

Gifford, John C., (ed.). *Billy Bowlegs and the Seminole War.*
(Dewars Limited Editions, Coconut Grove, FL, 1925).
Reprint of contemporary account.

Hassler, Warren W., Jr. *With Shield and Sword.* (Iowa State University Press, Ames, Iowa, 1982).
General U.S. military history including Seminole and Blackhawk wars.

Holland, James W. *Andrew Jackson and the Creek War: Victory at the Horseshoe.*
(University of Alabama Press, 1968).

Jacobs, James R. *The Beginning of the U.S. Army 1783-1812.*
(Kennikut Press, Port Washington, NY, 1947).

Lord, Walter. *A Time to Stand.*
(Harper & Row, New York, 1978).
An exciting popular history of the siege of the Alamo.

Martyn, Charles. *The Life of Artemas Ward, the First Commander-in-Chief of the American Revolution.*
(New York, 1921).

Potter, Woodburne. *The War in Florida.*
(University Microfilms, Ann Arbor, MI, 1966).
Eyewitness account of the Seminole Wars.

Smith, William. *Expedition Against the Ohio Indians.*
(University Microfilms, Ann Arbor, MI, 1966).
Reprint of eyewitness account.

Starkey, Marion L. *A Little Rebellion.* (Alfred A. Knopf, New York, 1955).
Shays Rebellion.

Sugden, John. *Tecumseh's Last Stand.*
(University of Oklahoma, Norman, OK, 1985).

Tinkle, Lon. *13 Days of Glory: the Siege of the Alamo.*
(McGraw Hill, New York, 1958).

Tucker, Glenn. *Tecumseh, Vision of Glory.*
(Bobbs-Merrill Co., New York, 1956).

Utley, Robert M. and Wilcomb E. Washburn. *The American Heritage History of the Indian Wars.*
(American Heritage Publishing Co., New York, 1977).

Index

Page numbers in *Italics* refer
to illustration